Cold

Also by Victoria Dougherty

The Bone Church

Essays on Love, Faith, Family
and Other Dangerous Pursuits

Cold

**VICTORIA
DOUGHERTY**

Cold

Text copyright ©2016 by Victoria Dougherty

Cover design copyright ©2016 Jennifer Zemanek, Seedlings Design Studio
Typesetting by Chris Bell, Atthis Arts LLC at www.atthisarts.com
Photos by John Michael Triana

All rights reserved. Except as permitted under the US Copyright Act of 1976, no part of this publication may be reproduced, stored in a retrieval system, or transmitted in any form or by any means electronic, mechanical, photocopying, recording, or otherwise, without written permission of the author.

Published by Wilderness Press

ISBN (paperback) 978-0-9974657-0-9
(ebook) 978-0-9974657-1-6

Visit the author at www.victoriadoughertybooks.com

Cold: The way revenge is best served; the way a war was fought; the way a story should be told.

[contents]

Born Cold . . . 1

[about my people]

The Best Worst Thing . . . 5
That Cursed Ruby Box . . . 11
When Pigs Fly . . . 15

[world without pain]

Why A World Without Pain Is A Wasteland . . . 21
Why I Love Czech Women . . . 25
Pain-Envy And Other Afflictions Of The Fauxletariat . . . 32

[to understand poetry]

Prague, My Alma Mater . . . 39
Running Away From Home Does Not Burn Calories . . . 43
The Trouble With Apartment A . . . 46
Pollution And Fog . . . 48
On Making A Man . . . 51

[despite everything]

A Wife's Ode To The Cocktail Hour . . . 59
A Few Words On Love And Valentines . . . 62
Why Despite Everything I Still Love Cigarettes . . . 66

[love the wind]

Home, Home On The Free-Range . . . 71
Wonderland City . . . 77
Faith And The Nine-Year-Old Skeptic . . . 81
Reading, Writing, And Arithmetic . . . 84

[power of art]

An American Tale . . . 91
Memories And Memorials . . . 96
A Candle For Dina . . . 99

[served cold]

James Brown Is In My Hot Tub . . . 107
Hard-Boiled Thrillers, Noir, And The Belly Laugh . . . 110
Bill Withers Is Still The Bomb . . . 112
Want To Understand Marriage? . . . 114
A Seven Year-Old's Thoughts . . . 119
Dracula: The Gothic Pimp . . . 122
Jan Saudek: The Straight Robert Mapplethorpe . . . 125
The Lost Art Of The Bad Family Photo . . . 127

[don't laugh]

Life In A Haunted House . . . 131
The Santa Quandary . . . 135
New Year's Wisdom . . . 138
Odd Little Post-Mother's Day Thoughts . . . 144

[love the grit]

Snowy Days Amidst Love And Death . . . 149
Heartland . . . 153
My Kind Of Town . . . 158

[having it all]

Sundays With Merle . . . 165
What's In A Name? . . . 170
The Never-Ending Surprise Party . . . 175
Flat-Out Love . . . 180
Why We Need to Laugh at Everything . . . 185
Only God Could Have Created Christopher Hitchens . . . 190
A Long Day's Journey Into Light . . . 194
On Love and Forgiveness . . . 199

[the ultimate expression]

A Case For Sorrow-Loveliness . . . 205
Truth, Beer, and History's Massive Tailwind . . . 210
The Bone Church: Real and Imagined . . . 214

[when we dance]

State of Grace . . . 219
Faith's Little Deaths . . . 222
Greed, Envy And The Berlin Wall . . . 228
August In The Cold . . . 231
Please Stay For The Fireworks . . . 234
The Meaning Of Happiness . . . 238

Born Cold

When I was a kid, watching ABC After School Specials was where middle class youth with troubled families could find themselves. On most Wednesdays at 3:30 pm, alcoholism, divorce and every day dysfunction were portrayed by actors like Scott Baio. I'm sure "The Boy Who Drank Too Much" was a real comfort to teens struggling with a drinking problem, and a good morality play for those who weren't. I liked them as much as anybody, but for my parents and grandparents, the "problems" portrayed on the ABC After School Specials were a real head-scratcher.

"Heavy drinking isn't problem," my grandmother would say. "It is part of life. Now dictatorship! That's a problem!"

If I wanted to see a more accurate reflection of what real problems were like, I should watch *Dr. Zhivago*, my grandfather once suggested. And I did—getting the same, satisfying recognition that most of my friends could find by surfing the networks. Varykino felt like home, even if I didn't live in a frozen summer palace, but a 1960s style two-story house in suburban Chicago.

And like Zhivago's, our family story was a two-hanky drama: heroes and villains, cowards, redeemers and the redeemed, those who were beyond hope, and those who pulled victory from a hat just as it looked like it was all over for them. There were ghosts, there were priests, and there were spies. Beautiful women and dashing men. Achingly beautiful love stories and wretched marriages. Drinking and smoking and storytelling—lots of storytelling.

"Did you hear about Uncle Jaroslav?" Heavy sigh, deep pull on a Carlton 120 (the "healthy" alternative to Viceroy in our household by the time the 1980s rolled around). "He hung himself in his shed." My mouth drops open. "Why, Baba?" My grandmother waves her hand—smoke goes curling around my poodle's head. "Why not?" she says.

I loved that woman.

And I love the stories I grew up hearing at my dinner table. I love black and white films and photos. I love the smell of whiskey and cigarette smoke on a man. And I love a tailored suit. I love rich, world-weary laughter, and a home with scratches on the wood floors and books piled up all over the place. Strong tea is good. Strong coffee is better. A strong man is the best. An old map of the world pinned to the wall—and two tickets to Buenos Aires in the top drawer, just in case. I love unpolished nails, but a nice coat of lipstick on a pair of parted lips—but lips not too full, like Angelina Jolie. More like Juliette Binoche. I love the rain. I love the cold.

And if you share the love, keep reading.

[about my people]

The Best Worst Thing

I *always* knew something would happen to one of my children. I never said it out loud. I didn't allow myself to dwell on it. But the feeling was there: a vague superstition that visited me on my paranoid days, the kind of day that would find me in my children's rooms at midnight, making sure they were still breathing.

Some of this superstition is in my heritage; I'm from a long line of Slavs, from what used to be Czechoslovakia, where a lot of people believe in curses. But my fear is bolstered by the fact that both my mother and my mother's mother have lost children in devastating ways.

Sixty years ago, my grandmother daringly escaped from postwar Czechoslovakia to join her husband, who had defected in Switzerland with some teammates from the Czechoslovak national hockey team, only to be foiled by the Communists from reclaiming the three daughters they had left behind (my mother and two aunts), who were then ages six, four, and six months.

Children were frequently secured in those days through neutral intermediaries, but in her case, because of my grandfather's high-profile defection, the Czechoslovak government put its boot down. As a result, my grandmother wasn't able to see her children again for two decades.

By that time, my mother, who was the oldest child, had already lost her four-year-old son, Victor, when he died from the flu — a victim of poor medical care in their tiny Czechoslovak village. Months later, with my surviving brother in tow, she risked prison and the threat of machine guns to escape to the United States, where she gave birth to me.

Our tradition holds that curses come in threes. And while the change in geography was a definite improvement for our family, I feared that the curse couldn't be far behind. So I waited my turn.

When it came I knew it would be something of biblical proportions, on par with swarms of locusts or the earth swallowing me whole — something I wouldn't be equipped to handle. After all, I was no freedom fighter or border crosser. I was just a middle-class girl from the Chicago suburbs.

I was sure my soft American life would be my undoing once it was my turn to share some family anguish. It had already taken its toll on my relationship with my mother, creating a gulf between us we couldn't seem to bridge.

My girlfriends spent hours on the phone with their mothers, gabbing about everything from job woes to weight gain, whereas my relationship with my mother seemed to consist mostly of awkward lunches that started with a bang of best intentions, but quickly fizzled, often ending mid-meal with her saying, "Well, got to go . . ."

I wondered if it was a cultural thing. As a child I was embarrassed by everything about my mother: her accent, her conservative political views, her va-va-voom beauty, her flashy sense of style, and the way she dressed me like an off-the-rack hybrid of Elizabeth Taylor and Ivana Trump. At her urging, I even received the sacrament of confirmation with a full face of makeup and red fingernails.

But our chasm went deeper. Behind my mother's

high-pitched giggle and enormous rhinestone brooches, under her Cleopatra-style cosmetics and bold, animal-print pantsuits, was a remove and sorrow I could never penetrate.

It was a result of years of being stalked by the Czechoslovak secret police, of missing her parents, of being forced upon resentful relatives, and, more than anything, of not being able to save my brother.

I had often tried to get her to talk about it. I wanted to know who my brother was and, more importantly, get closer to her. But she always shut me down. "You have no idea," she would say, ending the conversation. And she was right, because even after becoming a parent myself, I couldn't — wouldn't — comprehend what it felt like to lose a child.

Until last year.

A little more than halfway through my third pregnancy, my husband and I learned that our baby had a rare tumor on her tailbone. In a matter of weeks it grew so large and distinct within me that strangers asked if I was carrying twins. By my last trimester, the tumor was the size of a basketball and had begun to compromise the baby's kidney and liver functions.

When the doctors could wait no longer, Josephine was born by Caesarean section seven weeks early. She was not breathing on her own. Less than an hour after her birth, she was rushed into eight hours of surgery.

Her surgeon was able to remove the mass and reconstruct her bottom, and we hoped that would be the end of it. But it wasn't. As it turned out, Josephine's tumor wasn't benign, as originally predicted, but aggressive and cancerous. In the months following her birth, she would survive five surgeries and several rounds of chemotherapy that began roughly around her original due date.

The curse had arrived, and it was a doozy. But the earth didn't swallow me whole. I was neither too soft nor too weak to handle it. I was able to keep standing and be there for my daughter for one simple reason: my mother was there for me.

My husband often travels internationally for work and was in India when Josephine's tumor was discovered. I called my mother not to ask for help but just to tell her. At that point the doctors hoped the tumor would stay the nice, safe size of a lemon, or at least wouldn't grow any bigger than a grapefruit.

Regardless, my mother immediately packed, left her home and job in Chicago, and drove through the night to our home in Virginia. As Josephine's tumor doubled in size weekly and her condition worsened, my mother's visits became more frequent and more essential. She helped me stir oatmeal when the pain in my back kept me from standing at the stove; she took my children to the park when I had a hard time walking; she rubbed my feet at night the way my husband would have if he had been there.

After her birth, Josephine had to be operated on and treated by specialists at the Children's Hospital of Philadelphia, and during that stretch my mother bunked with me at the Ronald McDonald House. Eight weeks later, when Josephine was transferred to University of Virginia Hospital in Charlottesville, VA., my mother moved in with us and stayed for months.

Despite a heart problem, she kept late nights at the hospital, staying with Josephine so that I could care for my two other children. She tended to Josephine's surgical scars and cared for her ostomy with the expert hands of a nurse. At times she stared so fiercely into Josephine's eyes that I thought she alone was keeping my daughter alive.

She cooked and cleaned our house when we didn't care if we ate or if toys littered our living room. She laughed with us. She even told stories about my late brother, a topic that hadn't been broached since that last time I had tried to get her to talk about him, in 2001.

One night, after we caught my son playing "target practice" in the bathroom, aiming his urine at imaginary bull's-eyes and hitting everything but the toilet, she said: "That's nothing. One time I found your brothers shooting the pee at each other like they were shooting the gun — bang, bang! Having two boys, there was always something funny."

Later, she told me that after Victor died, she couldn't even understand how the sun could be shining; it made no sense to her. It was the first time she had ever spoken to me this way.

It sounds strange to hear myself say it, given the pain and turmoil of Josephine's battle, but my mother and I had a wonderful time. We cooked goulash together and spoke in our first common language, Czech, instead of lazing into English when we didn't feel like summoning a better translation of our feelings. We became experts on the ways of The Force, watching *Star Wars* movies over and over with my two older children.

My mother got to know our friends and became a part of our community. And as our friends got to know her better, they remarked on how similar we are. For the first time, this observation didn't leave us looking warily at each other, perplexed and uncomfortable.

The behind-the-back hand gestures I had once employed to signal to friends "Don't mind her, she's a little crazy" have been replaced by a desire to hold her hand as we walk along the street. I'm no longer embarrassed when my mother gives my friends "the lessons in the life" (as she puts it) by extolling her love for Richard Nixon, her favorite American president.

Josephine's illness may well be part of a curse, but it is still the best worst thing ever to happen to me. While robbing me forever of my peace of mind, it has given me my mother.

And it has made my mother a member of our family. She has gained the adoration of our little ones, whom she routinely piles into her car for outings to Toys "R" Us (or Dhoy-Za-Roos, as it is now pronounced in our house). She has a daughter who is her new best friend. Most of all, she has Josephine.

I'm still too superstitious to declare victory, but it looks as if my daughter is going to make it. If so, Josephine will have broken the curse and at last brought a mother and her child together in our family, instead of inserting a painful wedge.

My mother and I were talking about my late brother a few weeks ago. It was near Victor's birthday, which has always been a difficult time for her, a time when she normally would have withdrawn and hid from everyone until the day passed. But not this year. She was too busy assembling my son's Millennium Falcon Lego model brick by brick, and painting my three-year-old daughter's toenails a tarty red.

As she cut the tags off a hot-pink leopard snuggly she had bought for Josephine, her eyes began to fill with tears. "For forty years I had a hole in my heart," she whispered. "And now that hole is filled."

That Cursed Ruby Box

In the family I grew up in, love was often misplaced, nearly always badly botched, but nevertheless there—taking us from day to day. As a unit, we had every kind of bad luck you can imagine—Nazis, Communists, deaths big and small, petty humiliations and feature-film-worthy fiascos. It's luck so bad my mom actually calls it a curse. She believes that curse started germinating right around 1939—when Hitler rolled into Prague. My mom curses that day.

But I'm an American. The only member of my family actually born here and raised with the corresponding happy-go-lucky spirit that all of us Americans share to some extent, even the grumpiest of us, the most self-loathing. I guess that's why my family's story—from my point of view—didn't begin with "the curse." It began with a gold box with a big plastic ruby on it.

My grandparents had a tiny closet in their bedroom when I was growing up—maybe half the size of a shower stall. It was a place I liked to go when nobody was home, because I feared I would get in big-ass trouble if I was caught snooping around in it. Not because my grandfather kept dirty magazines there (I wished), but because it was where my brother, Victor, was kept.

His ashes sat in a dark bronzed metal container on the middle shelf of a metal-framed display case, surrounded by things that had meant something to him in his short life—a blue teddy bear roughly the size of a man's hand, for instance. He was also surrounded by things that meant something to my mother—a yellow vase filled with dried flowers, a small, iron crucifix. I was intrigued by the trinkets and tchotchkes. They seemed to burn with hidden meanings and when no one was around, I would take the tchotchkes down from the case and look at them.

One afternoon sometime after school, my grandmother finally caught me. I started explaining and before I knew it I was telling her all about how I'd come up there because I wanted to add something to my brother's shrine. I was just looking around for a good place to put it, since there was already so much stuff up there, I told her.

"What do you want to put there?" she asked.

"My ruby box."

A little gold box with a fake ruby on its lid—I used it, quite literally, to hold my fantasies. Maybe it contained a simple bag of wishes on one day, or a hidden message the next. Anyway, I did not want to put my ruby box up there.

"Are you sure?" my grandmother asked. She knew I really liked that box.

"Mm hmm," I said, praying she'd drop it.

"Okay, then," she said. "Go get it."

I went to the bedroom she kept for me in her house and took my ruby box out of my underwear drawer. I put the box right in front of the container with my brother's ashes.

My grandmother then kissed me and brought me downstairs for some Pepperidge Farm cookies.

I still really wanted my box back—especially when I remembered that I'd left a faux pearl ring in its belly. My only consolation was the tiny tickle of virtuousness I felt about having given up my ruby box for the brother I'd never met. And I guess I also hoped that in a weird way, my gift would forge a connection between me and my mom and my surviving brother that hadn't existed before, and really wouldn't until years later when I nearly lost one of my own children. My mom and my oldest brother had gone through Victor's death together—and in the old country. They shared that bond. I was born a year after Victor died, and in Chicago. And despite the shrine in my grandmother's closet, my brother was hardly ever mentioned and I knew better than to bring him up.

And now he had my ruby box. With my ring in it.

Over the days, that thought began to drive my eight year-old mind crazy. I started sneaking up to the little closet again. I'd pick up my box, open it, put the pearl ring on my finger, then take it off and put the box back. I was terrified that if I actually took the box back into my possession that I'd get cursed somehow. After all, what kind of jerk takes a present back from her dead brother? So, I'd pick it up, put it back. Pick it up, put it back. This went on for a couple of years.

But over time, the box lost its meaning to me and I stopped obsessing about it. I can't say I forgot about it entirely, but I definitely put it out of my mind for about thirty years. It only came up again because I was going through a pretty horrible time myself after my youngest daughter was born so sick.

My mom and I got really close then, and Victor stopped being a taboo subject. I'd become a full member of our tribe—the secret initiation being basically a catastrophic curse of an event. One that had been commonplace for the other members of my family, but had eluded me because I'd lived a very privileged, middle-class American life free of dictators, gulags, political prisons and the resulting havoc they can wreak.

"I remember when you gave Victor your box," my mother said, out of the blue. I'd had no idea that she even knew about it, let alone remembered such a thing.

"I didn't want to," I told her, and she smiled and said I could take it back if it was that important to me.

"Neh," I said. "He can keep it." We both laughed.

Maybe that box was the beginning of my part of our curse. Maybe I should rue the day I ever placed it in my brother's shrine, tossing my lot in with the rest of my family. But I don't. Because along with the heartache, and the begging, the sleepless nights, and the maddening loss of control that came with my part of the curse, there also appeared a few tiny cells of magic.

Grimm's fairytales have long told us as much. A curse is an enchantment. It does, after all, take more than a few historical events to transform a run of bad luck into a true curse. It takes something special—like fairy dust or spittle from a gargoyle, if I believed in such things—for a mere awful event to enter the realm of the supernatural. The way it might take a golden box with a plastic ruby to make a family out of a broken band of immigrants.

When Pigs Fly
Thoughts On Slavs, Santa And Eating The Family Pet

Let me tell you a little bit about my people.

Slavs are salty. Playful but intense, eccentric. We thrive on poetic double meanings, and can be as dark as we are passionate and sentimental. We believe in curses and we believe in that tiny, niggling feeling—the kind that prophecies are made of. The soul's equivalent of that barely detectable scratch in your throat just before a debilitating bout with the flu.

We've brought the world bawdy intellectuals, literary janitors, scientist priests, and philosopher politicians.

And we are warm. We welcome our guests not with a shake of the hand and a cold drink, but a kiss, an embrace, a plate of hot food and a glass of strong liquor that burns as it goes down.

I'm writing this essay at Christmas time, and about this time of year I get sentimental about being a Slav, because, well, I'm an American. I married an American guy and my kids can butcher all of about three Czech words (my fault, I know). We do the Santa thing—Christmas morning and all that. And I'm not complaining. Santa is probably the best mythical character ever invented, inspiring millions of parents each year to feign his existence in order to give their children a little bit of magic. That, as far as I'm concerned, makes him about as close to real as you can get.

But I do miss my Czech traditions—and not despite the fact that they sound so weird to Santaphiles, but because of it. Our myths and holiday customs embody all the bewildering contradictions of the Slavic race.

We scoff at Santa, but convince our children that a golden pig will fly across the night sky to signal the arrival of their gifts on Christmas Eve. Said gifts are delivered by none other than the baby Jesus, who most Czechs don't believe in anyway.

We are, sadly, an agnostic lot.

Our Christmas dinner—eaten on Christmas Eve—is not the lavish spread we'll whip up for any old Saturday night, but a humble meal befitting the simple carpenter in whose honor it's eaten. Carp soup, carp filet (baked or fried), and potato salad.

Though many of us despise our traditional Christmas meal, we eat it with a reverence left over from our staunchly Catholic past. It's eaten for tradition, but it's also consumed with a certain feeling of sentiment for the dark gray bottom-feeder that spent the last few days of his life swimming in our bathtub. A defacto member of the family, he'd been named, talked to, fed. How many kids get to watch their mother chop the head off their beloved new pet, and then eat it?

And if we're Christian by birth, we go to midnight mass. Hell, if we're Jewish by birth, we probably go, too. Just in case.

I remember one midnight mass in the St. Vitus Cathedral in Prague when the priest officiating berated the congregation for nearly three-quarters of an hour for being terrible Christians. Despite the fact that the house was packed to a standing-room-only crowd, he made the reasonable assumption that few of those present were actually people of faith.

Such is the contrary nature of the Slav. We're too darned left-brained to submit to something as subjective and intuitive as faith, but too superstitious not to show up at mass on Christmas Eve.

"A maddening people," my husband says. But he loves us anyway, and has always been a really good sport about the fact that nearly all holiday dinner table talk starts with some older relative's thousandth retelling of his time in the gulag. But it ends with boisterous laughter—most of the time. Or a ribald joke, regardless of how many tender, young ears are present.

We come from a tough part of the world, historically speaking—and we can talk about it. We can laugh about it, too.

In that spirit, I'd like to end with a quote from Adolf Hitler, if I may:

"Slavs are a mass of inborn slaves . . . all of the Slavs, especially the Poles and particularly the Czechs are an inferior race and need to be ruled with an iron fist."

To that I say, Merry Christmas, Mr. Hitler. I'd offer you warm grog and a bowl of goulash, but I'm an American—so you can bugger off. And Merry Christmas to anyone reading this. God Bless you. I mean it.

[world without pain]

Why A World Without Pain Is A Wasteland

Some years ago I attended an Easter brunch at the home of some friends of my parents. It was a warm, wonderful occasion filled with people I'd known all my life, and who, through their example, had somehow always managed to make a better person out of me.

I was seated next to a young man named Tim, who I hadn't seen since he was yea-high—cute and rambunctious, covered in some form of dirt from head to toe like most little boys. But by the time this Easter brunch rolled around, Tim was a man in every sense of the word—a U.S. Marine, in fact, who had recently returned from a tour in Iraq. A husband.

It is the tradition in Tim's family to do military service before embarking on a career in law or medicine. In Tim's case, he'd been planning to start law school in the fall, and a family with his wife, Kelly, right away.

But soon after his return, Kelly, who had been complaining of headaches and blurred vision, was diagnosed with an inoperable, terminal brain tumor. Lovely, bright twenty-four-year-old Kelly.

Within a matter of months, she was gone.

"It's downright un-American," a friend had told me just a couple of months earlier, after our baby was diagnosed with a tumor in utero. She was being ironic, but her point was made to me days later by a doctor who said with a completely straight face, "I can only imagine how you must be feeling. You must be asking yourself, 'how could this happen to someone like me, who is educated and . . . '" He searched for the right word, but failed to find it, letting his sentence taper off.

I knew the word, though. The word was entitled.

Entitlement is something with which I've always had a complicated relationship. I most certainly feel a great sense of entitlement—no doubt about that—but what complicates things is that I know what the other side is like, too. I did, after all, grow up in a family whose problems began with capital letters: Communism, Russians, Germans, Nazis.

The women in my family smoked their 120 cigarettes and drank their tar-black coffee while they talked about Stalin as if they'd known him personally. The men talked very little unless you asked. Their pain was exhibited in their complete absence of self-pity, their sense of duty, and their wry smile. To this day, due to my family's influence, I cannot bear a whiner.

So, that doctor was wrong about me. Sort of.

But he probably wasn't wrong about most of the folks he has to break bad news to. Many of us Americans, regardless of race, gender and socio-economic background, feel a considerable sense of outrage when it comes to hard luck. If you have any doubt, just try to explain to a mother from a famine-ravaged nation that the poor in our country are overweight and often have televisions, cell phones, and designer sneakers. We Americans have always had a different definition of what constitutes quality of life than much of the outside world—and thank God for that. It has raised the standard for the world at large.

But there is a dark side to the way we flinch from pain and tend to scream "It's not fair!" like an adolescent when things go tragically wrong. If you spend your life running from pain, you never get to experience the elegant beauty in grief, the myriad of blessings you can receive if you open your heart to whatever gut-wrenching experience has been visited upon you.

Let me be clear, I've hated every morsel of pain that I've ever had to choke down. And if I think I can avoid pain, I don't just do a side-step, *I run like hell*. I hate that my daughter was born anything less than perfect. I hate that Tim had to lose Kelly and all the dreams they'd planned for their life together.

I can't speak for Tim, but I know the pain I've had to endure has given every bit as much as it has taken away.

I now understand why, despite the political oppression my mother experienced in communist Czechoslovakia, despite being orphaned and left in the hands of cruel and resentful relatives, despite being thrown in prison for trying to escape to America, despite the death of her son, she continues to believe in the good of humankind, and often with more passion and faith than someone who has led a much easier life. It is because part of what comes with pain is the sweet knowledge that there are people you hardly know who come to your aid and save your life, that you have been dragged kicking and screaming into being a better person, and that whatever peace of mind you lost has been replaced by a gracious acceptance of whatever life has to offer.

It is why the slum-dwellers in India smile. It is why the Jews are famous for their sense of humor and the Slavs for their unbearable lightness.

It is perhaps why Tim approached me as I was leaving

Easter brunch, took my hand and said, "We are so sorry for you and your baby. Kelly and I pray for you every day."

I was speechless. "Thank you," was practically all I could utter. We, at least, had hope. He and Kelly had none. I did manage to tell him he and Kelly were in our prayers, too, and he smiled and thanked me as well. "We're just so grateful for every day we have together," he said.

Part of me would welcome a world where great people like Tim and Kelly didn't have to experience such a living nightmare. A world where only the sons of bitches got it in the neck.

But then I'd have to ask myself, what kind of world that would be? A world lacking inspiration, perhaps, resilience, growth.

Pain, aggressive, circumstantial pain (not to be confused with ennui), forces an answer to one of life's most fundamental questions: What would you do if the worst thing you could possibly imagine happened to you?

It can be a horror to contemplate—no doubt.

But the truth is, in pain there is a purposefulness in every waking hour.

Without pain, the world would be a single-celled organism. It would be the vacuous smile of a beauty contestant, the tiresome political rants of a news junkie, the pretentious ramblings of an artiste.

All day, all the time.

So, ask yourself this: could you even bear it? And wouldn't you, in a world without pain, just want to kill yourself?

Why I Love Czech Women

I was raised by two beautiful, captivating, and gloriously insane Czech women—a mother and a grandmother, who my husband affectionately calls "The Gabor sisters." As in Zsa Zsa and Eva Gabor (who are actually Hungarian). For those of you scratching your heads, Google them. It's worth it.

As I was growing up, what struck me most about my mother and grandmother, apart from their uber-dramatic lives and their goonishly big-hearted gestures, was that neither of them thought "the rules" applied to them.

My grandmother had come to the USA in the early 1950s—not exactly at the pinnacle of the women's movement—yet in my more earnest years, when I demanded to know what discrimination she'd suffered as a woman in the workforce, she looked at me quizzically.

So, I sang a few lines from a Dolly Parton song about workin' nine to five and hardly gettin' by cause they use your mind and they never give you credit and all that.

My grandmother still didn't get it.

Finally, she lost patience with me and said, "Look, wherever I work, within five years I was always the boss of men."

Gulp.

And it was *true*!

Even by today's standards, my grandmother had an

amazing career, running the business ends of three five-star French restaurants simultaneously. These were places that used to host Studio 54 regulars like Mick Jagger and other people my grandmother wasn't particularly impressed with.

It's not that she maintained discrimination against our sex hadn't existed in her day—she was sure it had. She just didn't see what that had to do with her.

I really couldn't tell you why, exactly, the glass ceiling was more of light mist for her. On paper, she was an immigrant woman who came to America at twenty-eight years of age with ten bucks between her and my grandfather and no English skills.

I can only say that my grandmother carried herself with a dignity and authority that said "watch out."

Some years ago she even recounted to me a story of a millionaire boss who up and confessed his love for her one day after work and begged her to run away with him. She told him in no uncertain terms that she was a married woman and that if he continued to behave in this way she would be forced to find other employment.

Of course, he apologized profusely, pleaded with her to stay, and the incident was never mentioned again. Until my grandfather found out and asked her to quit that job.

Which she did, moving onward and upward.

But I don't mean to imply that her rise was always paved with rose petals. My grandmother was once fired for being Czech. She was working at a brokerage firm where she became, characteristically, the "boss of men."

Until the Hungarian uprising of 1956.

A spontaneous, nation-wide revolt against Soviet policies, it was the first credible threat to the USSR since the end of the Second World War. Thousands of civilians were killed and it was a crushing defeat not only for Hungarians, but for democracy.

And the Czechs hadn't stood with their Soviet-occupied counterparts. In fact, Czech tanks—on Soviet orders—made their way into Budapest.

When my grandmother went in to work after this development, her boss screamed for her to get out and never return.

Devastated, she wandered outside, where she bumped into the owner of a rival brokerage firm and told him what happened. Long story short, she was hired on the spot because that broker had heard stories of how good she was—ironically, from the man who'd fired her.

My mother, on the other hand, has always been the queen of the get-around.

Though a valued employee, she didn't have quite the high-falutin' success my grandmother enjoyed. She did, however, manage to get away with murder in other areas.

To my knowledge, my mother has never parked in a legal parking space. What is extraordinary about her experience isn't her blatant flouting of the law, but the fact that she has never, ever, not once, paid a parking ticket. The tickets she has accrued have always been dismissed, ignored, or torn up on the spot. In one case my mother waltzed out of her workplace to find a police officer actually putting his own money into her meter. Not finding anything in the least bit strange about this, she thanked him cheerfully, then drove away.

My mom can haggle her way into a discount for a designer dress at Saks Fifth Avenue that she couldn't otherwise afford. She can get her hands on a brand-new computer for a pittance. Whatever it is, she can find her way to it, around it, on top of it, through it, or dig her way to the other side of it.

And though she is charming as hell, her way with a smile and a well-placed compliment doesn't begin to make clear her ability to get what she wants so much of the time. If it had merely been good looks and flattery, that wouldn't explain why, at seventy-plus and up about forty pounds, she can still get the same results. I'm telling you, after an apocalypse, I'm sticking with her.

As a kid, I thought this *Twilight Zone*-y mind over matter experience was specific to the women in my family—you know, like having blue eyes or being left-handed. But once I moved to Prague and met other Czech women in their natural habitat I wasn't so sure . . .

But I'll let you decide.

The following are a list of six basic traits that have come to my attention over years of observing and interacting with women of the Czech persuasion—including, but not exclusive to the women in my family.

1. Czech women are babes:

> Don't take my word for it. Just check any list of supermodels, either from today or yesteryear, and you'll find a disproportionate number of Czech women on it. Anyone from 80s sensation Paulina Porizkova to more modern day gals like Eva Herzigova, Eva Poloniova, Karolina Kurkova and so on and so on. My own husband can barely breathe when riding the Prague metro because of the bevy of beautiful women around him. Our son is already lobbying for a year abroad at Charles University there—and he's only thirteen.

2. Czech feminists look at things a little bit differently than their American (or British) counterparts:

> A Czech girlfriend of mine, a passionate feminist with

a PhD in biochemistry and a minor degree in Hindi that she got just for fun, I guess, once said to me, "Why do American feminists despise men? Don't they enjoy making love?"

I nearly choked on my Pilsner.

Consequently, when Czech feminists start talking about, well, feminism—the equality and possible superiority of women on both an intellectual and sensual level, the need of women to be heard, respected, whispered to, worshiped and given equal pay and a fair representation at the highest levels of industry and government . . . Well, let's just say that by the time we get there, even the most hostile-to-the-concept alpha male will lean in and say, "I'm a feminist, too." And he will mean it.

3. Czech Women (including intellectuals, artists and women on the mommy track) are sexy dressers:

I've known quite a few Czech female intellectuals (and they don't mind calling themselves such), and not a single one of them dresses like a frumpy schoolmarm. Case in point, the above mentioned friend spoke her observation about American feminists with full lips painted in lipstick, a cigarette, a short pencil skirt, and a tight shirt that showed off a fabulous chest. It would never occur to her that such an outfit might render her "less serious," and her many professional accomplishments seem to agree. My fellow Czech mothers are never opposed to short shorts or stiletto heels—sometimes even worn together and while pushing a baby carriage (I kid you not—I've actually witnessed this on more than one occasion).

4. Czech women win every argument:

> And they'll use any method within their arsenal to secure victory. This, of course, can be an unfortunate trait for those who love them or even cross their paths, but it's one to be admired nonetheless. They don't do it by shouting, or brow-beating or God forbid, withholding affection, but through a labyrinthine sequence of manipulations that leave their opponent scratching his (or her) head and wondering what happened. Yes, they are the women literature warned you about.

5. Czech women are natural athletes:

> Again, just look up any old list of Wimbledon Champions, gold-medalist skiers, etc. For such a small country, the amount of world-class female (and male) athletes the Czech Republic produces is pretty amazing. Is anyone reading this old enough to remember how Ivana Trump skied backwards while berating her then-husband, Donald, over his tawdry affairs? You don't want to mess with that.

6. Despite a penchant for six-inch heels, Czech women are outdoorsy, even back-to-nature types:

> A Czech woman will strip naked and dive into any old trout stream, climb a tree or chop one down if she has to. My own aunt can field-dress a bear while wearing a push-up bra and rhinestone earrings. It may not be blind luck that Czech Supermodel Petra Nemcova survived the tsunami of 2004 by hanging on for her dear life as a death current of debris rushed by her. Petra's boyfriend, sadly, did not make it.

Czech women—no matter how pretty—are tough.

Now, I'm not saying that all Czech women have all of these qualities. In my own family—as far as I know—we have no supermodels. And my mom actually hates the outdoors. My grandmother, while she lived, wouldn't be caught dead in pair of stilettos. But I have noticed a preponderance of these traits in women born in the Czech lands. And you have to admit, if you came across a woman with even some of these attributes, you might just put your arms in the air and back up—your heart pounding—and say, "Easy, lady. I don't want any trouble. But I wouldn't mind just a little . . . kiss."

Pain-Envy And Other Afflictions Of The Fauxletariat

Bedriska, my grandmother, was an elegant, aristocratic Ilsa Lund type, the kind of woman a man would do anything for. The kind of woman who would've made him do it, too.

My mother, Jirina, or Georgie as she calls herself in America, is gorgeous and vivacious. She is a Bond girl with a thick accent and a touching sweetness. A woman with a spine of steel and a broken heart. James Bond would've loved her—but like all the women he loves, she is a tragic heroine. If she and James had ever crossed paths, she would've ended up being fed to sharks by a villain with an even thicker accent then hers, or would've at least faced a tearful goodbye with her handsome spy, who couldn't bear to be with her for risk of putting her in harm's way.

These are the women of my family. They have fled across armed borders, hidden Jews, learned they were Jews, had guns held to their heads, have known how to double-cross and have known how to cross their legs to get you to notice.

So, it's no surprise that I grew up with a touch of pain-envy.

The three-hanky movie played on at home while I went to Catholic school, staring out the window and dreaming about spies and adventure. To my family's credit, they were far more interesting than any of the subjects in school, or even most of my friends, for that matter.

And I was left recounting my family stories to my friends. It seemed important somehow.

At what we called "the swamp"—an empty church parking lot and hang-out for pre-driving rebels—I had a captive audience. A lot of my friends were punk-rock wannabes who drew "tattoos" on their arms with red Sharpies and had no interest in realpolitik. But despite the Lucky Stripe cigarettes that dangled from their black lipstick-painted mouths, their defiant poses, and self-styled Mohawks, these were good kids who didn't want to hurt my feelings.

They knew our family had seen rough times even if I hadn't.

As I grew up, my family's experiences began to have a profound effect on the way I viewed my own life. When faced with the onset of middle school politics, I couldn't help but think of what my mother's seventh grade experience was like. There is something about the onset of sixth and seventh grade that turns sweet, if precocious, young girls into monsters. Mean girls would taunt and torture me and I would retaliate in kind, hating them and myself during the process.

My pity parties, however, were always busted up by the knowledge that when my mother was twelve, the mean girls she contended with could've had her or her remaining family members arrested if she misspoke, and they were egged on by her very own teacher, who openly called my mom the daughter of capitalist pigs. Pigs who loved the prospect of money in America more than the dream of building a socialist utopia in the Eastern Block. More than they loved her. Never mind that my grandparents didn't leave their home country willingly. If they'd stayed, they would've been thrown in prison on trumped-up charges.

Don't get me wrong, my mother was never one of those mothers who told stories of her hard luck childhood in order to shame me or make me grateful for what I had. Maybe that's why her stories were so effective. She told them out of pain and anger—when she told them at all—and in the process put a damper on my teen angst.

As time went on, she also unwittingly helped me shed any left-over traces of the pain-envy I'd experienced in my early teens. So much so that I grew to have a particular distaste for that affliction, even if I understood it all too well. Pain-envy breeds a sense of moral superiority within its sufferers, often accompanied by at least a trace of hypocrisy, and an uncontrollable desire to make the afflicted the hero in his own story—even at the cost of the truth.

I've seen it present in large portions of the populace—in places like San Francisco when we lived there. The fauxletariat—my husband actually coined that term—would walk around in their shabby clothes and three-hundred-dollar hiking boots aching for the hardship of a third-world garment factory worker. Sure, they wanted to make the workers' lives better, and that's a great thing, but it was more than that. They coveted the depth they believed people who have suffered—really suffered—accrue.

And there is some truth in that.

Except for the pesky fact that for every person who has experienced pain with a capital P and becomes more sage, kinder, almost glowing in their life force, there is someone who, although also having been visited with agony, remains petty, mean-spirited, foolish, even downright silly.

We have plenty of both kinds in my family.

So, I leave pain-envy for the fauxletariat. The people with mostly intact (or intact-ish) families who didn't grow up with moms obsessed by curses and "Red brain-washing." Their moms, like the moms of my friends, worried about whether they wore helmets, if music needed a warning label on it for violence and sexual content, if internet predators lurked in every chat room. All good things—I'm not knocking them. I shopped for two weeks to find the best skateboarding helmet for my nine-year-old daughter.

Even if I know it's mostly emotional busy work that gives me a mostly false sense of security.

But I indulge myself in all the fixations of a happy wife and mother just like my friends' moms did. It is a privilege to have such small things to worry about. I know I will be lucky if my kids grow up only to envy pain.

But I do want to give them some balance—the kind I was fortunate enough to have.

I make sure to tell my children the stories I heard around my dinner table. I want them to feel close to those experiences and understand them deeply. I don't want them to feel far away, the way the plight of an un-free Tibet feels to an earnest college student. I want those stories to engender a sense of curiosity in my children that stretches beyond borders and partisan political beliefs.

It was, after all, my own family stories that made me sign up for the Greece and Turkey program in college and go backpacking through Europe, even if I couldn't really afford it. They were what inspired me to sell my car and move to Prague for three and a half years, start my own business, and ultimately decide I wanted to be a fiction writer—as if there weren't enough of those in the world.

Those stories and the experiences they inspired in my own life showed me that pain wasn't something to envy and romanticize. It's an important building block of emotional and spiritual growth and I wouldn't trade mine, don't get me wrong. It's just that as much as I once envied the clarity and simplicity of the problems my grandmother and my mother had faced—the bad guy with a gun, the dictator/homicidal maniac who is intent on silencing every dissident voice and trampling over every right a citizen of any functioning democracy takes for granted—I don't want those problems, no matter how good a mind-movie they make.

I just want to write about them.

[to understand poetry]

Prague, My Alma Mater

For some people, their defining years were in high school: that first passionate kiss in the back seat of a Mazda; the artful way they managed to change the birth date on their driver's license—even if it only fooled one, old Asian man at a 7-Eleven across town; the weathered Jeep their dad bequeathed to them on their sixteenth birthday, essentially setting them free. Those things reshaped their lives and allowed them to see themselves anew. They were something to build on.

For others it's college: falling head-first into a first real love affair, the keeping-a-toothbrush-and-spare- change-of-clothes-at-their-place kind, of trying on the hat of poet, rock-n-roller (after all those humiliating years in Band), intellectual, or joining a fraternity or sorority and finally getting to act out all of the scenarios they'd been coveting in the movies.

For me, however, it was the time I lived in Prague.

Don't get me wrong, high school and college were great, and I would undoubtedly look back on those years with more than just a passing glance if I'd never sold my car, quit my job, and moved half-way around the world to the country of my family's origin.

But the fact is, the roughly four years I spent in the Czech Republic shook my life to the core, and forced a metamorphosis in me on par with Franz Kafka's, but without the tortured, want-to-kill-yourself-slowly aspects. He did, after all, morph into a cockroach.

I morphed into a daughter, a wife, a mother, and a writer.

If you define karma as Wikipedia does, "the principle of causality where intent and actions of an individual influence the future of that individual," then my time in Prague was filled with it—from my first job on the newly named Political Prisoner Street, a pretty powerful coincidence for a girl who came from a family of political refugees, to my translation of a Communist propaganda play that my theater performed to several full houses of howling Czechs, to the close ties I forged with a family I never thought I'd meet, and the friendships that will sustain me until my death.

I met my husband in Prague, while performing an original, naughty, comic-feminist poem I'd written for my friends' amusement. We were at a four-hundred-year-old candlelit pub, at a long wooden table filled with ex-pats. Months later, I would hear that after my recitation, my husband had turned to a mutual friend and asked, "Who is that?"

Our friend told him.

"Well, that's the girl I'm going to marry," he'd said.

It was a time so raw and invigorating. And not just for me, but for everyone in that part of the world. The Berlin Wall had come down, the Velvet Revolution had transformed a nation without a shot being fired, a playwright had been elected president, and a lot of young people just like me had come to see what it was all about. I toured concentration camps, I slept under the stars on my father's farm, which had only recently been given back to my family through restitution (the process of returning property that had been stolen by the Soviet State), I worked for Czech companies, and I drank way more than I should have. I went to weddings and pig roasts—actually learning to make homemade sausage, though I've never used that skill again— I was chased down a dark alley by a Serbian gangster, I attended countless balls (sounds fancy, I know, but for Czechs it's more akin to dance hall culture than hoity-toityness), I saw a dozen or more operas for mere pennies, and I finally learned to understand poetry. Not by reading it, but by living it.

And in a few days I'm going to take my nearly thirteen-year-old son for week in my old stomping grounds.

Just him and me.

I can't tell you how nervous and excited I am.

My father has just negotiated a sale of his farm, and my son and I will be the last people in our family to see it while it still belongs to us. This is a house and a piece of land that has been under our care for well over three hundred years, minus the four decades under Communism. And now it will become a brewery and hops farm. Just like that.

I'll also be introducing him to a version of me he's never met: a woman who perfected the art of the smoke ring and French inhale, who can't quite remember how she got home some nights, who has stood on stage in less than her underwear, for heaven's sake, playing a harried newlywed in a Czech play.

While I'm hoping some of my more colorful antics won't be trotted out in front of the boy, I'm so proud to introduce him to my friends. These are people who are not only hosting us in their homes (no hotels for us!), but who went out of their way to set up and promote for me a reading of my novel, *The Bone Church*, at The Globe Bookstore and Cafe.

The Globe and I go back a long way, even if it's no longer owned and run by my homies.

This is a place I helped scrub and scrape for its opening some twenty years ago. It's also the place where I first seriously entertained the notion of becoming a professional writer—even if I never told anyone. Now, I wasn't one of those people who wore berets, talked about Kierkegaard, and nurtured a hostility towards the ruling classes. I had a day job supplemented with a night job in theater that actually cost me money. And I had none of the ennui necessary for a credible stab at the writer's life.

But somehow, here I am, taking my kid to a reading of my novel at a bookstore at my alma mater, the city of Prague.

How's that for karma?

Running Away From Home Does Not Burn Calories

When I was twenty-three years old, I moved to Prague, Czechoslovakia. I could say it was to meet my extended family who, until a few short years before I bought my one-way ticket, had been trapped behind the Iron Curtain—and that would be true. I could say it was because I loved adventure and Prague was the place to be at the time and that would also be true. I could say it was to get a greater understanding of my own family, but I'd be giving myself way too much credit.

Mostly, I moved to Prague to get away from my family.

I wanted to escape a loving but distant relationship with my mother, and a close, but blood-sucking relationship with my grandmother. And let's not stop there. I wanted to get away from the rest of them, too: my biological father, my adoptive father, my brother, and even my aunt way down in Florida—already a good three thousand miles away from my home in Chicago.

Even that wasn't enough.

It wasn't that I wanted to erase them from my life—in fact, most of my family, including my mother and grandmother, visited me while I was in Europe and I was happy to see them.

Very happy.

A friend of mine suggested that perhaps part of me thought I could avoid a certain strain of bad luck that seemed to follow my family like that piece of grungy toilet paper that sticks to your shoe after a visit to a public restroom.

But in truth, I ran from their love.

It was crushing, complicated, and carried a dark cloud.

So, with a twisted logic—the kind of logic that only makes sense if you grew up in a Slavic family—I left my Czech family for Czechoslovakia. It was the place they'd run from, the seat of our misfortune, and, I believed, my only salvation.

Czechoslovakia had risen anew, elected a playwright president, and was struggling to be what it might have been had the Germans never come and the Russians never stayed. That seemed like an apt metaphor for me.

My time in the old country was spent first as a tourist and later as a resident alien. I explored crumbling castles, worked in a Czech company, saw a full double rainbow on my father's farm, crouched inside the dungeon of Countess Elizabeth Bathori—known as Countess Dracula because of her penchant for drinking the blood of virgin peasant girls (they claimed to be virgins, anyway). I drank dark, caramel beer in a seven-hundred-year-old pub, observed midnight mass with a whiskey flask in one hand and a vigil candle in the other, and on Christmas, ate carp soup made from a fish that had been swimming in my great-aunt's bathtub that very morning.

Prague was and remains the place from where all of the good fortune in my adult life has come. I met my husband there, had my eyes opened to the world, and began my writing career. It was nothing short of magic.

Prague also grew me up and sent me humbly back into

the folds of those who loved me—even if they didn't always like or understand me. Even if their affections could be painful at times—even toxic. Three generations of damaged people living together and crossing each other's boundaries on a regular basis is nothing to romanticize, after all. I knew what I was getting back into.

But I couldn't, after walking to work on Political Prisoner Street, not think of my mother and her time spent under an unforgiving interrogation light. I could hardly visit my great-aunt, who had taken me in when I first arrived and who I had grown to love dearly, without seeing my grandfather's melancholy blue eyes in hers.

When push came to shove, by running away, I had come closer to my family than I ever imagined possible.

And when I returned home, some three years and change later, I was ready to curl up in their laps, take a drag of their cigarettes, and let them into my life in a way I had never done. Gone were the days of wanting to run screaming from every holiday dinner, refusing to find any humor in the motley crew of eccentrics gathered around our table, of being incapable of embracing gratitude for my own blessings. Ones of love, originality, and enough stories to fill volumes.

In running away, I found that I could shed nothing about my past, and more importantly, didn't want to. Home had become a state of mind, an outlook, a way of walking through life by cuddling its glorious insanity close to my chest like a one-eyed teddy bear missing half of its stuffing.

The Trouble With Apartment A

In Prague, I lived in a building that looked like a photo still from the 1949 thriller, *The Third Man*. Not enough light; the faucets barely worked; there was a weird film poster of *Nanuk of the North* left behind by the previous tenant. And I mean weird. Like a cockamamie merger of Eskimo soft-porn and man and dog buddy adventure. But I loved that place, and it still gives me chills thinking about it.

My little ground floor flat had all the creepy romance of an Alfred Hitchcock thriller, but without the style. I remember the way my neighbors used to spy on me. Really spy on me—eyes pressed to their peepholes. They knew what I was doing in real time and reported my comings and goings to my landlord with a scrupulousness that bordered on the insane—as in, "She carried her grocery sack in her left hand, although we know she is right-handed" (no joke). They called me the Amika—which is basically a slur for "American girl" on par with "guido," "spic," or "chink," according to my landlord, and were aghast at how many people were always coming in and out of my flat. Since many of my friends were guys, they naturally assumed I was some sort of hooker. In fairness, they simply had no imagination for the every-day-is-a-party kind of life that a post-graduate ex-pat girl in her twenties could enjoy—or that a lot of my so-called customers were gay. Actors from the theater I was a partner in, who came by to pick up a script, or complain about a director, or have a drink after a long rehearsal.

By day, my building was your typical, timeworn, turn of the century apartment house: swarming with left-over communist snitches, and in desperate need of some tuck-pointing and a decent paint job. But at night it transformed into a place of rough and tumble glamour. Echoes from the grimy, weed-infested courtyard included soulful melodies a housewife hummed from her garden flat window, some guy's perpetual, hacking cough, and racket from the neighborhood pub which filtered in from the pub's kitchen. It grew louder when the cook burst out of the backdoor to smoke. He'd leave the door propped open and a cacophony of clinking glasses, folk music, laughter, ribald conversation, and the occasional fight would float up and up and up—all the way to the top floor units, maybe eight stories.

My neighbors might have minded that I didn't use my dominant hand to carry groceries, and they might've minded my choice in friends—or that I had any friends at all, but nobody seemed to mind about the noise. We all knew that was magic. No matter how much we all hated that the hot water ran out before we could rinse the shampoo out of our hair, or that there was a weird fungal smell vaguely reminiscent of three-day-old dog poop that permanently infused the air; at night, we were living in a black and white movie and our conventional lives became mysterious, even exciting. An actor with a slight lisp and boyfriend trouble became a customer; a common tattletale became an agent; an aspiring singer perhaps a tragic heroine. And the coal-stained bricks and chipped tiles? Mere evidence of a life well-lived.

Pollution And Fog

If you're reading this, you may already suspect that I have a thing for noir. I love its style—the tipped fedoras, the fitted clothes. I love that a cigarette is more than a prop—it's treated like a piece of jewelry.

But in the few short years after the end of the World War II, when cool was being codified, Hitchcock's blondes were running amok, and French noir was coming of age in one part of the world, drab was not only being exalted in another part, but forced upon a populace. And it was only a few doors down.

I got my first up-close look at grim communist style when some distant relatives of ours escaped what was then Czechoslovakia and landed on our doorstep. This was about 1983. To describe them as bad dressers simply doesn't begin to catalogue what I can only define as a look of utter defeat. Hair not quite disheveled, but untended to—combed, but not washed, cut, but not in any particular style. Their clothes were also curious to me. Don't get me wrong—I'd seen a lot of awful get-ups in my day. I grew up in the 70s and 80s, after all. And I wasn't making some sort of stuck-up sartorial judgment. There's no other way to explain it other than to say that their clothes—the dreary colors, the awkward sweaters with lumpy shoulders and ill-fitting sleeves, the synthetic materials that not only trapped smells but managed to highlight every possible physical imperfection—they made me sad.

I didn't know then that this look was not specific to this family, but pervaded every aspect of life in the Eastern Block. It was as ubiquitous as sideburns in 1972, or as the *Friends* haircut in 1995. Only it persisted for forty years, and wasn't exactly a fashion choice.

I'd seen movies and countless old family photographs, so I knew what a sharp contrast it made to the down-but-not-out style of war-torn Europe only a few decades before. Back then the woolen caps, the cotton shirts, even the crumbling architecture managed to maintain a sense of dignity. Or at least a look of good times passed. It was the look of fog vs pollution. Fog can be cleared, but pollution leaves a layer of grime, a stench, a persistent cough. It just can't be fixed with a little bit of mending. It needs a complete makeover.

The cheerless fashions of Eastern Europe may have visited me in Chicago in the early nineteen-eighties, but I didn't get an actual look at what I came to call the architecture of despair until I went to Czechoslovakia for the first time in 1990—shortly after the Berlin Wall fell. Growing up in Chicago, I'd seen bleak housing stock, but I somehow wasn't prepared for the row upon row of apartment houses in outer Prague that stared ahead as mutely as a bad passport photo. The Section 8 housing in urban Chicago had at least earned its ugliness, but these vertical ice cube trays that stood tall in a bed of concrete—not a single tree in sight, or even an attempt at beauty—had arrived fully formed. As if this was the best it would ever be, was ever meant to be. The urine yellows, the tartar build-up browns, the dirty snow grays that gave every façade, hallway, and room a case of terminal ennui—those hues had been chosen on purpose.

Noir is black and white by style, but the communist style—with the exception of some brilliant poster art—made everything appear not like an old photograph, but a water-damaged one.

Vaclav Havel, the Czech Republic's famous playwright president, contended that there was an unmistakable connection between bad taste and bad government.

And I think he was right.

Style can be dangerous. It's sublime. A supreme expression of confidence and individuality—even in the worst of times. At its core, style is the ultimate expression of hope. And in noir, even the most doomed heroine will apply a coat of lipstick and fix her hair. Her clothes will be smart and snappy, freshly pressed. The most world-weary detective will put his collar up, tie his coat at the waist. Because there's always hope that the fog will clear by morning and that whatever they're doing is worth a hill of beans in this world.

On Making A Man

This is a year of milestones for my family. My husband and I celebrated our fifteenth wedding anniversary, the Velvet Revolution just marked its twenty-fifth anniversary, and our oldest child, a son, will be turning thirteen.

For those of you who may be a bit fuzzy about the Velvet Revolution, I'll give you a refresher course: The Velvet Revolution was a non-violent series of demonstrations in Czechoslovakia that culminated in an end to forty-one years of communist rule, followed by a peaceful conversion to a parliamentary republic. It was truly one of democracy's great days and one I can't look back upon without getting all *verklempt*. Not a single shot was fired.

As for the other two milestones, I think a fifteen-year wedding anniversary is pretty self-explanatory. But for those of you who don't have kids, I'll enlighten you a little bit about what it's like when the first one turns thirteen.

I'm sure you've heard, but thirteen is when all the fun begins.

Or not.

Given all that's at stake, it's crucial to me that we start the teen years off on the right track, and I decided that a mother-son trip back to the old country was in order. The country that I only narrowly escaped being born in— which, I like to remind my children, would have disqualified me from ever being president here in the US of A. That little civics lesson is an added bonus.

I was a bit apprehensive about spending a week alone with my son on a tour that didn't involve any of the usual activities that he values in a vacation. You know—beaches, fishing, and a lot of lounging around.

A trip to the Czech Republic is a very adult vacation. One filled with history and family. And in this case, one even infused with work. My son not only got to watch me perform a reading of my novel, *The Bone Church*, at a Prague bookstore, but listen in as I furnished a lengthy interview to Prague Radio that included a good deal of rather delicate family information he'd never heard before.

I knew our week would be jam-packed, exhausting and utterly alien to him. My hope was that my son could walk away from our week in Prague with something of his mother to take with him through his more challenging years. During a time when he'll be breaking away from my loving embrace, as he should, and taking his own counsel or the advice of his friends over mine, as he also should from time to time, and springing, swelling, sometimes snowballing into the man he will become.

I've given a lot of consideration to what kind of mother I want to be to my son. To the kind of man I want to raise and unleash on this world. I've thought about everything from discipline (I'm a fan) to independence (a necessity in my point of view) and character (absolutely essential). My husband and I once disqualified an excellent private school for our children when we learned about an incident where a bus driver had refused to drive an inch until an overly exuberant teen was able to control himself and sit down. We would've shaken the man's hand, but the school gave the driver a pink slip after the disruptive and disrespectful student's parents complained.

I just want so much more for my children than a culture of entitlement and a single-minded obsession with self-esteem. Especially when I've seen how in my own life, my sense of worth has come far more from opportunities to employ morals and principles, and an ability to acquire skills and sharpen talents, than even a thousand *you go, girls*. The fact that my husband and I love our kids beyond reason is table stakes. It's the other stuff that can be more challenging in an age when parents are terrified of not providing the perfect environment for their children's future success.

I suppose we're no different in that regard. We just go about things a little bit differently.

Believe me, we are not the kind of parents who fetishize the "good ole days" of child-rearing. We don't want to bring back the wooden spoon and tell our kids they'll go blind if they masturbate. But we also don't want them to grow into adults who believe the world will accommodate their every grievance. Or conversely, for obedience to be their defining characteristic because they've never been allowed to fail. We strive to create an environment where our children are allowed the critical landmarks of growth that come from making mistakes and getting into danger every once in a while. The kind of danger that comes from being permitted to ride their bikes unsupervised or watch a horror movie or settle a dispute without adult intervention. We don't always succeed.

In my own, crazy, Cold War family, I saw how vital it was to address important, scary, complex, and adult issues. To not shield children from the existence of death, evil and all manner of barbarity. These were talked about in great detail at my dinner table when I was coming of age, and those tales—far from scarring me—did nothing but deepen my empathy and enrich my understanding of humanity. Even if they did disturb me. Keep me up at night sometimes. Make me cry.

The world is a beautiful mess and my parents never tried to clean it up too much for me. Nor did they ever clean my room for me. That's been a positive force in my life.

So, back to our trip to Prague. I viewed it as a launching pad for my son's young manhood and a vehicle for our relationship to make the adjustment from "mommy and me" (okay, he hasn't called me mommy for a pretty long time now), to just "me and mom."

Our relentless, almost psychedelic trip to Prague came on with gale force wind—beginning with catching a Czech film about the Prague Spring as it was being shot. A lucky break, we ran into a film crew as we strolled around Vinohrady, where we were staying, and got to pose for pictures with vintage cars, tanks swaddled in fog made from machines and actors who were costumed in late 1960s groovery.

We walked until our feet ached, trolled the castle dungeon and its accompanying torture museum, and shopped for souvenirs on the Charles Bridge. I let my son ask me anything he wished about marriage and sex; about our friends who had gotten divorced and why. He even got the opportunity to hear his grandfather tell the story of his and my mother's defection. How, like in the movies, my father found himself crawling in the grass only to come nose to toe with a pair of boots, then look up into the eyes of a border guard and the barrel of a gun. It was a first for me, too, as I'd only heard the story from my mother's point of view.

I took him to my mother's village to stay with family

friends—warm, kind people who treated us like their own, and strolled with him around our family farm, which had recently been sold to a brewer. Sprawling and once stately, it had been in our care since before the American Revolution. And now, it was gone.

At home, my son dresses like his friends—terribly. I mean truly—with unkempt, unwashed hair, pants that are either too big or too small, t-shirts and dirty underwear. He's a sartorial disgrace and he knows it.

"Part of the herd, Mom," he says.

But in Prague, he allowed himself to look great. His hair was washed and finger-styled. His clothes were neat and masculine. He even let my friend Beth dress him in a vintage coat and tails with a tie pin for a night on the town. He stared at himself in the mirror and saw the man he will one day be.

"Wow," he said. "I look good."

And on our last night, I took him to an authentic, French burlesque show.

Along with my two equally middle-aged girlfriends, Nancy and Beth, we dressed him up, teased him, let him take a ceremonial sip of beer, and educated him about the style of theater he was viewing. And don't worry, moms and dads, it was all tastefully done. He's seen more skin on his friends' moms at our local pool than he did at this very chic and sophisticated burlesque show. He just loved that while he was the youngest one there, he still wasn't treated like a kid.

The next morning, as our plane began its taxi down the runway, my son looked out the window and said, "Come on, Mom. On the count of three—goodbye, Prague! We'll miss you."

I swear, my heart skipped a beat.

I'm hoping that our son's passage from boyhood to manhood will be as peaceful as the Velvet Revolution. I would like the inevitable transition of power to go without bloodshed, police intervention, or too many tears. But I don't want it to be easy for him, either. Or easy for us. We don't grow that way. Or at least don't grow enough. Sometimes we need the trouble of a rough and tumble journey in order to become anyone worthwhile. A guy a girl can depend on, a friend can respect, and a child look up to. You don't become that man without having to defend yourself or others, break a heart, or have a heart broken for that matter. And it's a journey that for the most part, a boy has to make on his own terms.

[despite everything]

A Wife's Ode To The Cocktail Hour

My husband and I had a lot of fun before we had kids. I mean *a lot*. We traveled, we spent money like crack whores, we had nooners, for God's sake.

And we also loved going out for cocktails. We probably met at some swanky bar or curious hell-hole or trendy hipster joint five days a week after work.

It was fun.

And least of all because we got a little loopy. The fact is that most of the time we really didn't. What we would do is laugh and talk and debrief each other about our days. Sometimes we had pow-wows about our dreams and where we wanted to be in five years. Or maybe we just chattered about where we wanted to go the coming weekend.

I always made sure to put some lipstick on and leave at the door whatever bad attitude I had brewing before I walked in to any of these establishments. I wanted my husband to remember why he married me and see a glimpse of the woman he first laid eyes on at a candlelit pub in Prague back in 1994.

It's like I always tell him, "The last twenty-five year-old woman you had was me." And I don't say it to depress the man.

When we had kids, we knew our lives would change, and we were ready. We understood that dragging a bunch of kids around the world was not only prohibitively expensive, but no fun. Kids want to go to the beach or to Disney World. And they will make you pay if you try to take them to, say, The Louvre. Nor could we lay around naked reading the newspaper anymore. Not unless we wanted to go to jail.

But my husband and I are pretty determined people and we were adamant about having a relationship that didn't exclusively revolve around family activities. We wanted to stay interested in one another and have a way of getting caught up on each other's soap opera.

So, we instituted a cocktail hour.

Every evening, before we set our sights on making dinner, my husband mixes us a great cocktail and we sit down on our porch or in my husband's office and get down to the business of making each other laugh, telling a story or sharing a great idea and trying to get the other on board. There are only two rules to our cocktail hour: no children allowed, and no talking about children allowed (unless it's a really great story).

And while the kids complain every once in a while, or try to crash our party, we're pretty emphatic about it. I once said to my daughter, "Would you prefer to live in a house where your mom and dad don't want to spend time together?" That was a revelation for her.

Over the years, I have to admit that our cocktail hour has caused a little bit of embarrassment in our small town. Our youngest, for instance, was charged at school with painting her daddy's "favorite things" on a flower pot as a Father's Day present. She painted nothing but martini glasses, and I'm sure that got a good laugh in the teacher's lounge. My son once took a message from a caller and said, "Sorry, but it's cocktail hour and you don't want to mess with that. My mom will call you back." The caller was—no kidding—his Sunday school teacher.

Our cocktail hour is worth a few wagging tongues, though.

It's a little wisp of a vacation at the end of the day. A mini-date that has acted as a daily reminder of how much we enjoy each other's company when we're not fixing lunches and feeling confounded by "new" math and watching *Young Frankenstein* for the 1500th time. It is what has helped keep our relationship a living, breathing thing—even if we're not carefree young adults anymore with stubbornly thin physiques and the confidence to smoke a cigarette without the fear of impending doom.

A Few Words On Love And Valentines

I've got some words from the late, great Katharine Hepburn that are just going to set your heart on fire.

In a missive taken from her autobiography, *Me*, she's actually talking about that cowboy of all cowboys, John Wayne. Not the love of her life, Spencer Tracy.

So, if you've got *Me* handy, go to page two-fifty-nine and damn, when you read those few pages on Wayne you might just have to take a cold shower and run out and rent about five of his movies. Even if you're a straight guy.

And I say this as someone who is not particularly a fan of The Duke, as he was called.

If you don't happen to have *Me* in your library, however, I'll give you the nutshell version.

She described Wayne as colossal and superhumanly masculine. With big blue eyes that scrutinized you and the world. Rugged skin lined from good times and big, hearty laughs. Sharp witted, too. Not the man of few words that he often portrayed on the screen. Gregarious. Fun as hell.

Hepburn attests to his massive chest - one she thrilled to lean against. And hands so huge that hers, when in his, seemed to disappear.

"So tall a tree," she said, "That the sun must shine on him whatever the tangle in the jungle below."

Yet despite being a long, tall glass of beer of a man, he was light on his feet. A wonderful dancer whose every move was marked with a delicate grace.

Wayne saw everything, listened to everyone, really concentrated on the matter at hand. He was self-deprecating, brave and charming as hell. "Knows it. Uses it. Disregards it," she said. "Dangerous when roused."

But she didn't stop there.

"Outrageous. Spoiled. Self-indulgent. Tough. Not much gets past him."

Katharine Hepburn defined him as the kind of man that legends really are made of. The sort who built this country, and was bold enough to seek greatness. He did it on his own. He did everything on his own. Never sorry and never feeling sorry for himself. Ever.

"He dares to walk by himself. Run. Dance. Skip. Crawl through life. And at the core, he's a simple and decent man. With an ability to think and feel."

Her description simply takes my breath away every time I read it.

It meant a great deal to me when I was looking for love, making me feel at once hopeful and silly and faithless and terrified. Not because I wanted an uber-mensch just like John Wayne, per se, but because Katharine Hepburn's description dares to ask a great deal of a man. Demands it, in fact. And requires even more of the kind of woman who might deserve his attention and devotion.

Love can be daunting. It can feel like it hits you too hard sometimes and leaves you exposed to the most wretched of heartbreaks. A guy might seem one way at first—a veritable Prince Charming frothing over with all the things you think you want to hear—but in the end he's a big fraud. Or simply fickle. Maybe you didn't live up to his expectations.

A girl might be shimmering with sexual allure but carry none of the attributes necessary for a friend. Or perhaps the woman who makes you feel as if you're going to burst into flames, who seems to understand your every thought before you give it voice, sees you as merely a buddy or confidant. That one stings like a nest of hornets.

There are so many varieties of love affair—each one a high-risk venture. They do call it falling in love for a reason.

Sometimes, it's just a matter of timing.

Like when I met this man years ago, long before I got married. I had just started a business and endured a painful breakup with someone who was almost right.

This guy was funny and confident and handsome and made the kinds of bold, romantic gestures that seemed dangerous. Way beyond the candy and flowers routine, he set about wooing me with a barrage of anonymous postcards—ones daring me to meet him in smoke-filled lounges with great jukeboxes. He swept me up for a champagne and fried chicken picnic on a windy hillside. And he was a corporation man—not what I was used to—who ran a simple telephone conversation like a meeting.

But he could quote everything from a Langston Hughes poem to the U.S. Constitution accurately and credibly.

It was when I was returning home from visiting him in the city where he lived, that I picked up a magazine at the airport and—seated uncomfortably between a Chinese student and big Chicago Bears fan—read my horoscope.

This is something I never do. But sometimes these rare impulses provide some insight.

It was one of those horoscopes that thinks it's really clever and insults you, and mine said something like, "You always think you have it all figured out and now you've finally met someone who doesn't swallow your B.S. and say it tastes like a cookie. And yeah, you might just have a shot at happiness. Question is . . . can you take it?"

Well, I decided right then that I could not, would not, and was not going to take it. Sometimes that voice tells you you're not ready. That there is, perhaps, a different sunrise out there waiting for you. One not so blinding. The kind that's bright and joyful, but is absent the violent bursts of color. And the potential for complete annihilation.

The following day, after my horrorscope (misspelling intentional), the guy with the postcards and the fried chicken called and asked me to come see him again.

I said, "Um, well, you know. I can't."

He was silent for a minute, then softly, he said, "Please."

Love is magic meets decision. I'm not sure if I read that somewhere or made it up.

It's refusing to settle and not being afraid to strike a bargain. Standing for something so that someone will stand by you. Never being a free lunch or accepting one. No matter how lavish the spread.

And love is a leap of faith—even when the timing couldn't be worse. It is, like John Wayne, being bold enough to run, skip, dance, crawl if you must. It is simple and decent. Thinking and feeling.

When you endeavor to fall in love, you must be willing to live and die entirely on your own judgement. Step out of the movie and go boldly into your life. And you must be ready to die a thousand times in order to chance living forever.

So, the answer is yes. I did go see him again.

And again. And again.

Why Despite Everything I Still Love Cigarettes

My husband has started smoking again.

Okay, this is nothing new. He stopped when I was pregnant with our now thirteen-year-old son and began again when our youngest daughter (now nearly eight) was born with cancer. The doctors had told us as much. They told us that people, okay parents, in the NICU (Neonatal Intensive Care Unit) tend to pick up old habits. Men and women who haven't touched drugs in fifteen years are found shooting up in the bathroom; former sex addicts will take a ride on any willing X-ray technician in one of the broom closets; svelte Pilates moms will gain thirty-five pounds in a four-and-a-half-week period, bingeing on ice box cake and Jell-O parfaits offered in the hospital cafeteria. Let's just say I wasn't surprised when my husband turned to me just after one of the more troubling diagnoses we'd had to endure, and said, "Don't judge me, please. I need this just to cope." He took out a pack of Marlboros, peeled one out, and lit up like he'd just gotten laid after six months in the desert.

I was upset, of course. I don't want my beloved to get lung cancer or any of the other insidious diseases that we all know cigarette smoking can cause. But I also understood—and I'd be damned if I was going to nag him about it.

So, instead, I leaned in and kissed him—taking a deep inhale.

I used to love the smell of cigarettes. More specifically, cigarettes and whiskey mixed together. For me, it is the smell of sex.

When my husband and I were first dating, he smelled of cigarettes and whiskey all the time. It may be one of the reasons I married him, if I'm to be completely honest. And while I was not happy at all about my husband compromising his health because of the trauma accompanying the birth of our daughter, or his subsequent inability to kick the habit even though our little girl has, by and large, recovered from the worst of it—his smoking habit lit a fire to my libido that baby cancer might have under most circumstances crushed. Cigarettes helped us continue our relationship as a loving, married couple in a situation that could have easily destroyed any romance that we might have desperately tried to conjure as we struggled to hang on to our faith and our sanity.

For that, I must thank the Native Americans for inventing this terrible habit, Philip Morris, RJ Reynolds and other such companies for selling it, and us masses for taking it up like the chumps we are.

Because, if it weren't for the cigarette, my husband and I might have lost each other. I might have crawled deep into myself and become a woman consumed by my struggle to keep my kid alive and be a decent mother to my older, healthy babies. I might have begun to look upon my husband as merely a partner in the basic survival of our family. He might have begun to look at me as someone who simply needed him to ensure our financial survival while I fanned the fires at the hospital and at home. That happens a lot to people under merciless, unremitting stress.

So, if you'll excuse me—I must go have a cigarette. Or at least wrap my arms around my husband's neck and breath in deeply.

[love the wind]

Home, Home On The Free-Range

This past week, all three of my kids contracted what I can only describe as the Pompeii of stomach flus.

I spent my week cuddling, medicating, holding back hair so it didn't get barfed on, doing laundry, obsessively washing my hands, tracking diarrhea footprints all over the house, taking temperatures, dispensing Popsicles, rubbing tummies, detoxifying bathrooms, and wrapping blankets around shivering, feverish second, fifth, and seventh graders.

I'm not asking for sympathy here. Not much, anyway. As a parent, this is what I do, and it's both a responsibility and a privilege.

There's a sweetness to caring for my sick children. It's not just their helplessness and return to calling me "Mommy" again, even after a significant reprieve. (Although that does hold a certain allure.) Somehow, they're at their most beautiful when they're really sick. Their pale faces glow like the full moon, their lips are pink, dry and swollen, and their eyes glassy, sleepy and filled with love and need.

I could stare at them all day.

Of course their breath is deadly and their body fluids disgusting; they're also crabby and demanding and milk the whole sick thing for longer than necessary—not to mention making it damned near impossible for me to get any work done, and prompting me to post a picture of Sylvia

Plath with her head in an oven on my Facebook page. Cheap laugh, I know.

Finally, after eight days of this, I put my foot down and refused to cancel dinner plans my husband and I had made some weeks ago. I'd been looking forward to this date all along, as it also involved friends with whom we can have great conversations without having to edit the content, you know what I mean? And by the time last Saturday rolled around, this date wasn't just something I wanted to do, it was something I needed in order to stop myself from running away from home.

I knew that leaving for a couple of hours was iffy. Not in terms of my kids' safety. They were over the hump, and my oldest is extremely competent and just a month shy of turning thirteen.

But although they were definitely on the mend, my middle child was still weak and weepy.

She begged us not to go.

"Honey, I'll do what you want," my husband said. "But she'll be okay. We're just down the street and all she's going to do is lie here and watch TV anyway."

I knew he was right. I'd been at her beck and call day and night for what felt like a century and a half at this point. There wasn't anything left to do but wait this out.

So, I tucked my little girl in, put the phone by the couch, stuck a movie in the DVD player, kissed my youngest, who seemed to be thrilled we were going out (God only knows what she had planned), and gave my oldest instructions on what he needed to do if Mt. Vesuvius began grumbling again.

"Yeah, yeah, I know," he said.

It took my husband a full ten minutes to talk me down once we got into the car. He's great at that and has always been a huge champion of maintaining the integrity of our relationship. He's made me go away for weekends alone with him while I was still breast feeding, dragging my breast pump along like a third wheel, pulled babysitters off the street if need be so that we could get just a couple of hours together, and never had one qualm about being the bad guy when it comes to separating me from the fruit of my womb.

I love that about him. Even when I've hated it.

And overall, it turned out to be a pretty good night. We actually got through dinner until the inevitable call came. My daughter wouldn't stop moaning and my son was back on the toilet. So, we said our good-nights, thanked our friends for their understanding, and left just before dessert and espresso.

Once home, we nuzzled, kissed and put to bed our babes. It was all much ado about nothing.

Until today, when a friend of ours sent us a story from *The Washington Post.*

In it, a couple who practices "free-range parenting" was being investigated by DFS for allowing their children to walk home from a local park unaccompanied by an adult. The kids (ages ten and six) had been working up to this with short jaunts to the 7-Eleven and a neighbor's house. They were neither scared nor in danger of any sort when they were picked up by police, who were responding to a call from a local who voiced concern about seeing unattended children on the sidewalk.

The parents were outraged.

As young children in the 1970s and 80s, they had walked well over a mile to and from school every day. The father, a physicist, asked the social worker in charge of their case how it was possible to criminalize a parenting style, simply because it favored giving children freedom within a framework, allowing them to work their way up to responsibilities and liberties—much the way he had as a child. Is it illegal for children to walk home from a park less than a mile away in a safe neighborhood? Especially when they knew the way, could recite their address and telephone number and even had the self-awareness to tell the police officer who picked them up, "We are free-range kids and we're not doing anything illegal."

Until reading that article, I'd never heard the term "free-range" in this context, but it was impossible for me not to draw a connection between the philosophy behind the movement and my own attitude towards child-rearing.

My husband and I have tended to be consistently ahead of the curve when it comes to letting our children ride their bikes to a friend's house, or be responsible for themselves and even a younger sibling while we run some errands . . . or slip out for a dinner date.

We get as many raised eyebrows as we do pats on the back from like-minded parents or simply friends from a slightly older generation who feel all this helicoptering has gone too far.

"We're raising fearful adults who lack basic competencies," one of those friends observed.

He has a point.

Statistically, the world is a good deal safer—in terms of crime, at least—than it was twenty, thirty, even forty years ago, when a kid had mastery not just of his backyard, but his whole neighborhood. Back when it was common for a child, usually a boy, to wake up at zero dark thirty every morning from the age of eight to work his paper route . . . alone, and during the winter months, in the pitch darkness.

Pulitzer Prize Winning novelist Michael Chabon was

inspired by his own "free-range" childhood to write *Mysteries of Pittsburgh* and has said he would not have nearly as many stories to tell had he not been allowed to roam his home town and discover the world without interference. Through his wanderings, he created a vivid interior life, and earned the confidence to write several spectacular books about it.

My own childhood was filled with mystery.

I spied on creepy neighbors, walked a frozen creek alone for at least a mile, never once trick-or-treated with an adult, rode my skateboard down steep hills, played flashlight tag after nightfall. I remember being terrified, exhilarated, and bathed in utter abandon.

It was glorious and I knew it, even then.

I learned who to avoid and what intersections not to cross—all on my lonesome, or in the company of peers. And it gave me trust in my own abilities. I don't know if I would have had the guts to move to a foreign country or endeavor to become a writer had I not indulged in those tender-age freedoms first. Would I have earned the self-assurance and good judgment to fall deeply in love—as I did with my husband—and give my life over to the pursuit of our collective dreams? Hard to say.

Have I been in danger? Probably, yes. Maybe more than I realized sometimes.

I've lived in bad neighborhoods, traveled alone taking night trains, and met some bizarre, shady characters. Once, while visiting a friend at her college, my girlfriends and I chased down a notorious serial flasher with mocking taunts. He'd been plaguing the school for years and our performance made the cover of the school newspaper. I remember the headline read something like "Depravity Rocks Benedict Hall" and the student reporter posed as a classic flasher—complete with raincoat and sock garters—while the girls and I feigned looks of Puritan horror.

I wonder if, in today's world, that headline would have read, "Parents of Victimized Sophomores Calling for Investigation of Sexual Malfeasance at Local University."

But maybe I'm being too harsh in my assessment.

The fact is, we're all just trying to do our best, and parenting is a long, exhausting, joyful, and sometimes frightening trek. Whether you are "free range" or a "helicopter" in your style, your kids unwittingly become the focal point of your life. Your own happiness and well-being hinge both in the short and long term on their successful journey from child to adult.

And I'm sure kids from either type of home will probably turn out just fine, thank you very much.

So, I'll wrap up with what I think back on whenever I worry if I'm being too lenient or too interfering. It was something a hearing technician said to me in the hospital some seven years ago.

My youngest, who had been born with cancer, was having her hearing tested. A possible side-effect of one of her treatments was hearing loss, so I was waiting with bated breath as the technician finished his exam. He'd been having problems getting my infant daughter to respond on one side.

Finally, he looked up at me and said, "Don't worry, she's going to be okay."

I practically gasped with relief. "So, she can hear?" I said.

"Oh, I have no idea—the test was inconclusive," he said. "She's going to be okay because she has loving parents."

That was all I needed to hear.

Wonderland City

My husband was driving our seven-year-old home from school this past week and she rolled down her window, sticking her head out like a dog. Spring has come late and it was a glorious day. She was giggling and putting her hands up, lost in abandon.

"I love the wind," she exclaimed. "It blows you away to a wonderland city."

Sometimes her innate sense of poetry just makes me ache.

This is a child who slithers around the house in a mermaid tail. Talks to herself in a variety of characters and voices. She must be pried out of her fantasy world for dinner, to make the bus, to get dressed, brush her teeth, or pay attention in school.

I can't blame her. When I was a student my own fantasy world was far richer and more absorbing than learning long division, and my math grades reflected that. Sadly, so do hers.

Our ten-year-old is no less dreamy, even if a hot competitive streak does tend to keep her more engaged in school and extracurriculars. She writes stories and songs, loves drama class, paints portraits, makes "art" movies that include long pauses, sparse dialogue and heavy doses of ennui, and has great comedic timing, which she puts on full display at her elementary school talent show every year. Unlike her younger sister, she is nearly a straight-A student.

I say nearly.

Now let me share with you a conversation I had with her a few weeks ago:

Me: "We need to look up what course levels you were placed in for middle school."

Her: "Why? It doesn't matter."

Me: "What do you mean?"

Her: "I'm not smart."

Me: "What?"

Her: "I'm in the average math group and I get mostly Bs on my math tests."

Me: "Okay, so math is not your strong suit, but it wasn't mine either. Or you dad's. Doesn't make us idiots. I mean, I dunno, I think we've done okay."

Her: "Yeah, but you're writers. Nobody cares about writing anymore, mom. Or anything else. It's only math. If you're not great at math or into science, you're dumb. That's the way it is now."

Hmmm.

I guess we could have run out and gotten her a math tutor, pumping up her grade to an A and possibly qualifying her for the honors math she would need to ace in order to get into the more competitive schools later on. STEM (Science, Technology, Engineering and Math) is where it's at as far as our current educational industrial complex is concerned.

But we didn't do that.

It's not because we didn't want to invest the money or the time in order to give our daughter every possible advantage. Our monthly output for enrichment activities alone is like a mortgage payment. When push came to shove, our decision not to press our rising middle schooler harder was actually quite practical.

Math is simply not her strength.

If she was getting a poor grade, then certainly we would do something about it—but a B+?

Already, she's gotten the impression that any career outside of STEM is risky, unwise and unneeded. My husband and I have kibitzed ad nauseum with each other and fellow parents about our children being under far more academic pressure than we ever were—and at a much earlier age. So, finally, we decided to put actions behind our objections and resist reinforcing the pressure at home.

Don't get me wrong, going against this massive tide is exhausting and feels self-defeating at times—and we're just at the beginning stages. The compulsion to help our kids achieve, achieve, and achieve is great. We've gone back and forth about how to approach our children's respective educations and by no means do we claim to have the right answers.

In our case, we just felt that if we sang along with the STEM chorus, my husband and I might be playing a role in pushing our daughter into a career where she might do fine but never truly shine or feel the level of satisfaction that we feel every day when we sit down at our desks. A belief that we're doing what we're best at, what we are meant to do, has nurtured a zeal for our work that has helped us remain faithful during economic downturns. It has enabled us to shake off disappointments and defeats that might have prompted others to throw in the towel.

As we looked soberly at our daughter, it occurred to us that her energy might be better spent on becoming great at the subjects she excels at and loves, rather than merely good at the courses that feel like a dentist appointment to her.

Don't get me wrong, we don't have a damn thing against STEM. Our son, our eldest, fits like a glove into this STEM-oriented system. This is a kid who orders owl pellets off Amazon at his own expense and dissects them for fun, plucking out the animal bones and reconstructing a full skeleton of the varmint the owl had for supper.

More power to him!

And we're well aware that historically, girls have gotten the short end of the stick when it comes to STEM.

But a lot of that has changed dramatically over the past generation. Several of our daughter's close girlfriends are tracking into STEM, so I doubt she's lagging in the subject because of gender bias at school.

Math just doesn't appear to be where either of our girls' heads are at, or their passions for that matter. And we would no sooner push them to marry a man they don't love because he seems like a "good provider" than we would try to force them into disciplines or careers that feel closer to tasks than callings.

Life is too short and professions require too many hours for that.

And if our girls' interests change—fantastic! We'll switch up their summer schedules to include calculus camp in place of the art camp they beg us to enroll them in year after year. We'll break out the dusty chemistry sets they got from my dad for Christmas a couple of years ago and let them blow up the kitchen. We'll even rip down their posters of the Eiffel Tower and Ariana Grande and replace them with ones of MIT and Stephen Hawking.

Until then, we're okay if they prefer wearing mermaid tails in wonderland city to white coats in laboratories. HG Wells, after all, inspired generations of scientists and inventors with just a pen and an imagination.

And maybe math wasn't his strong suit, either.

Faith And The Nine-Year-Old Skeptic

I love our church.

It's a Cistercian monastery that sits with the most beautiful pastoral view of central Virginia and is lorded over by an intellectual priest and a body of warm, pious nuns who always make our children feel not only that they are welcome, but that everyone there is giddy for their arrival.

It's the only church I know of where the Easter Sunday sermon references Nietzsche and "Perpectivism." I didn't know what Perspectivism was until this past Sunday, but it basically means that there are many possible truths. And it was a perfect introduction to the nut of the sermon, which centered around faith: its meaning, its contradictions, its place in our lives, its tenuousness at times, its controversies.

It was also an eerily appropriate follow-up to a conversation I had with my middle daughter, my nine-year-old, Charlotte, the night before, as we were sitting down to dinner at a "fancy" new hamburger joint. (By fancy, I mean they serve alcohol as well as milkshakes.)

My husband and I had just taken our children to see the new, re-envisioned biblical epic, *Noah*, and my daughter had some issues.

Aside from the fact that Charlotte really hated the movie, which she called "dark" and "mean," she also confessed—for the first time after years of Sunday school, Catholic masses, and getting her sweet cheeks pinched by the above nuns (whom she loves), that she sees "absolutely no proof for the existence of God." Furthermore, she feels her Sundays are wasted by Sunday school classes that teach a concept she doesn't even believe in.

I was at first tempted to counter her smart-aleck tone with my own and say something like, "Yeah, well I don't know if organic food is any better than regular food, but I still pay twice the price for the fruit I put in your lunch box." But something stopped me.

Perhaps it was the hand of the God my daughter denies.

Instead, I told Charlotte that doubt was a part of faith, not separated from it. Faith, I said, is about believing despite the absence of hard evidence one way or another. It's how we go about love and art, which we also can't prove. Love is an act of faith. Art, both creating and experiencing it, is an act of faith and interpretation. And I also told her that it's her journey, not mine, and I'm not forcing her to believe. I'm just giving her information, and—if she's interested—my point of view.

She was *not* interested in my point of view. So, I dropped it. She'd attended a sleepover party the night before and had a grueling soccer match that afternoon, so I knew she was tired and crabby and not exactly in an open-minded mood. I did slip it in there that she still had to go to Sunday school, though.

"I figured you'd say that," she said, barely above a whisper.

Charlotte is our most intellectually restless child.

And she is also our most fragile.

She has a heart that she can barely contain, and wears it on her sleeve, her lapel, the buckle of her shoe. For her, a B+

is equivalent to failure, and the slightest hint of a reprimand sends her bottom lip into a quiver. She's overly generous to both her friends and her enemies—a trait that has been pointed out by every one of her teachers. Charlotte is most proud of winning the good citizenship award at school.

And I fear that, more than any of our other children, she needs faith—an internal resource that will be there for her when we can't be.

Charlotte sat on my lap for most of Easter mass. As we stood and recited the Rites of Baptism—as is the custom on Easter—she held my hand and looked at me as she gave her responses.

Do you believe in the God the Father, almighty, creator of heaven and earth? I do, she said.

Do you believe in Jesus Christ, his only son, our Lord, who was born of the Virgin Mary, was crucified, died, and was buried, rose from the dead and is now seated at the right hand of the Father? Again, I do.

Do you believe in the Holy Spirit, the holy Catholic Church, the communion of saints, the forgiveness of sins, the resurrection of the body, and life everlasting? I do.

This is our faith. This is the faith of the Church, we are proud to profess it, in Christ Jesus our Lord. Amen.

She probably didn't mean it.

I knew she was trying to please me, and she did, but not for the reason she might think.

I was pleased because of the almost unbearable love I feel for her. I was proud of her independent nature and innate skepticism. She always thinks things through before drawing a conclusion.

And I was happy—for her—that she wasn't quite finished thinking through faith, despite her assertions to the contrary on the night before.

Reading, Writing, And Arithmetic
(Scratch The Last Part)

I'm not by nature a prolific reader. A prolific imaginer, yes, but reader? Hmm. I'm slow, I'm picky, and I tend to want to turn everything into my own tale.

I can't remember a time when I haven't preferred the sanctuary of my own private, sometimes weird library of mind-stories to the extensive and fully utilized library my husband and I share in our home.

One that includes everything from literary classics (all the usual suspects befitting a lit major, from Herodotus to Franzen) to agonized Eastern European poets and writers that any self-respecting Slav must possess (Milosz, Kundera, Dostoevsky) to tasty genre specialists (Tom Rob Smith, Laurie R. King, Stephen King, Silva, Ludlum, Hiassen) to downright cotton candy (EL James, David Lee Roth's rock-n-roll memoir *Crazy From the Heat* and let's not forget *Rock Star* by Jackie Collins, a personal favorite).

I have read most of them—swear. Except for some of the less exciting business books my husband collects—*A Brief History of the Boeing Company*, for instance.

It's not that I don't enjoy reading—I do, and very much. Rather, inventing stories as opposed to merely savoring them just offers me a more three-dimensional experience—sort of like working a crossword puzzle, eating strawberry shortcake and listening to Dusty Springfield all at the same time. Heaven.

And once I had kids and my time became more precious, I had to pick a team. So, I chose to spend most of my time writing.

But in the last couple of years that's changed a little bit.

Since joining an online community of writers—a group of slightly pathetic if lovely individuals, who don't usually leave their homes except to tend to basic needs, and may not even get up from their computers unless they absolutely have to go to the bathroom or something—I've been forced, as both a professional courtesy and to avoid seeming like an idiot, to amp up my reading time.

As a result, I've strayed way far out of my usual interests, diving head-on into paranormal erotica, gushy romance, hippie-lit, and contemporary drama. All of which I would have passed by in the book store in favor of a great thriller or engrossing historical novel.

And besides giving me the pleasure of immersing myself into someone else's story for a change and getting to relax and put my feet up, it's also taught me a great deal about reading itself and has made me more aware of my own mind. Actually finishing books that aren't my cup of tea—that I would have surely put down were it not for the fact that I had promised the author I would read his work—has expanded my universe of interests. There's something about having to reach a story's conclusion—like it or not—that opens your heart to the author's intentions. It's like making yourself listen—really listen—to the other side of a political debate.

So, yes, it has made me a better reader and writer, but I'm not going to bore you too much with that cliché, because in all honesty, it hasn't changed my approach to writing all that much. At least not in the way teachers and writers will contend, insisting that you simply can't be a real writer without being an avid, even obsessive reader. I've never quite bought into that particular myth.

What reading more has done for me—a most unexpected and glorious blessing—is actually far more personal than professional. It has helped me maintain a strong bond with my children as they've begun the move from childhood to full-on teen-dom.

Now that my older kids are readers, I can share more with them than merely the content of their days. I can learn what inspires them, the kind of love they want to find, the friend they want to be, the daydreams they have about if their wildest dreams come true.

Reading what's on their Kindles has been a window into their worlds—one made of stained glass. I get to share with them books we end up loving together—*The Book Thief, The Apothecary, The Hunger Games, How We Fall,* and ones where, perhaps, we appreciated where the author was heading, what she wanted to accomplish with her story, but it wasn't quite the journey we wanted to be on. *Twilight* comes to mind (no throwing rotten tomatoes, please—we're not haters here). And then there are the novels I tried to get them into but failed completely—like *Harry Potter* ("Sorry mom, wizards freak me out") and Bram Stoker's *Dracula* ("Just don't groove on vampires, you know?").

As a mother, reading has helped me understand my children's thought processes, allowing me those rare glimpses behind the mask of shrugs and dismissive "fines" and "I don't knows" that follow any question about how they're feeling. I've noticed, for instance, that I haven't heard the words "You just don't understand!" in a pretty long time.

Reading YA, especially, has brought me back to my own

youth and reminded me of how raw, confusing, dramatic, hopeful and harrowing growing up can be.

And how magical if it's done right—wandering the woods, jumping on trampolines, just dying to meet Taylor Swift, playing doctor.

That has been a splendid realization, and one that reminds me that no emotion is trite when you're feeling it for the first time.

So, there you have it.

Reading more has not necessarily made me a better writer. And I'd still rather write my own story than enter someone else's. But what reading more has done for me—with an emphasis on reading fiction—is what it has been doing for human beings since the dawn of the written word. It has helped me connect with others—particularly those most dear to me. It has reawakened parts of me that I'd long since forgotten about, put aside in my busy life. And it has helped me understand the plight of my fellow man better than a thousand diversity seminars.

[power of art]

An American Tale

I know——the state of politics in the land of the free and home of the brave has got us all depressed. The Left and Right can't get along—on the political stage or the home front—and it's just causing us all a lot of heartache and embarrassment.

In light of that, I've been thinking a lot about my own family, how we got here, and why we love it—even in times like this. I thought I might write a little bit about that, if for no other reason than to get us all talking about America in something other than political terms. America is, after all, a concept, a philosophy, a great experiment.

As recent immigrants, my family's story is fresh and real—told by the same people who lived it. That in itself is a blessing, really. Sometimes a curse, too, but mostly the best thing that's ever happened to me. It has helped me evaluate my own life as I walk, skip, do the fifty-yard dash, sometimes hobble my way through "the great journey," as somebody great once called it. I would have never met my husband—in the old country, as luck would have it—had my mother not dragged her pregnant derrière across dangerous, armed borders and made her way to America—or as we say in my family, "the best darned country in the world."

Now, don't go getting offended if you're either not American and happen to think your country is pretty darned good, too, or if you're one of those self-loathing Americans who hates to sound full of himself. My family owes the US of A a lot, so we've earned the right to our starry-spangled-banner-eyed opinion. It's kind of like me saying that I've got the best husband in the whole darned world. It's a subjective statement brought on by loyalty, gratitude, faith, and flat-out love. Not arrogance.

And getting here, according to the people in my family who actually got here, was not a foregone conclusion. In other words, nobody woke up one day and said, "I think I'll go to America," got on a plane, and *voila*!

It was *hard*. It took a hell of a long time in some cases. And it required a level of courage and faith that most of us hope we never, ever have to demonstrate.

Yet some might say it was in the cards all along. And I'm willing to go along with that, too.

About a year before the Prague Spring (round about 1967), my Aunt Viki visited a fortune-teller. She wasn't the kind of fortune teller who had a tent, a crystal ball, and charged a fee in order to impart what your Uncle Louie wants to tell you from "the great beyond."

She was simply a little old lady who lived in a cold-water flat beneath my aunt's studio apartment in Prague. There was nothing "woo-woo" about her—she was just able to read your fortune from an ordinary deck of playing cards. Two of hearts, nine of clubs, etc.

If she liked you.

Well, she liked my aunt and one day she sat down to a cup of tea with her and got out the old playing deck. My aunt really only had one question for her—Will I ever see my parents again?

You see, my grandparents had fled Czechoslovakia twenty years earlier under threat of arrest.

They weren't knocking off liquor stores or anything. During the war, my grandparents had helped people—mostly Jewish—get out of the country to safety. Theirs was no Oscar Schindler story—they only helped a handful of people: the boyfriend of a neighbor and the family of an Embassy official—but it was enough, after the communists seized power, to get my grandparents into trouble.

Despite the Soviets' own complicated relationship with their German predecessors, they were not fond of people who would risk their lives for their principles or endeavor to break the law in any way. The Soviets liked their people compliant, morally vague, and easily frightened.

So that's the part that gets my grandparents into heaven. The murkier part, the part that lands them in purgatory for a few thousand years (if you believe in such a thing), is that they left their daughters, ages six, four, and six months, behind.

It was a devastating mistake.

While it's true that it would have been difficult to get them across the border, it's also true that the girls were harassed and harangued by the Czechoslovak government and treated appallingly by their own extended family. Their life in communist Czechoslovakia was nothing short of a tragedy and I can't, as a mother, imagine doing what my grandparents did—or worse, doing it and then having to live with it.

As my mother has pointed out, during the horrible years of World War II, women often chose to go with their children to the gas chamber rather than live without them.

But a child's tie to her mother is no easy thing to sever.

My aunt wanted desperately to see her parents again—especially her mother. Even if she could scarcely remember her. She wanted to understand why they did what they did. She wanted out of Czechoslovakia—a country she felt had betrayed her, filled with a people she found weak and corrupt, and run by a government she thought bankrupt in every possible sense of the word.

So, she sipped her tea and asked her friendly neighborhood fortune teller if she would ever see her parents again.

The old woman dealt several cards from her deck, laying them on her table. She stared at them for several seconds before locking eyes with my aunt.

"Yes," she said. "And soon."

But she didn't stop there.

"You will move to America," she told Viki. "There you will meet a Czech man, like yourself, marry him, and give birth to two children. After the birth of your second child, you will become very rich."

"But first," the old woman cautioned. "There will be a terrible tragedy in your family. A child will die a needless death."

Two weeks later, my four year-old brother, Victor, would die of the flu. His death would set off a series of events that would change the entire course of history for my family. It would bring my mother and surviving brother to a new country, put a long-overdue death knell into my parents' truly horrible marriage, reunite my mother and her sisters with their long-lost parents, and finally, bring me into the world.

It is a horrible price to pay for a new start and a new life.

As for my aunt, you may wonder if the rest was true. Did she marry a Czech and get rich after the birth of her second child?

That story goes something like this: at a dance for Czech immigrants about two years into her life in America, my Aunt Viki did, in fact, meet my Uncle George (a fellow

Czech immigrant). They moved from Chicago, to Iowa, to Florida, and did, in fact, have two boys. As Viki was recovering in the hospital from her second childbirth, she called out to my uncle.

"Hey!" she said. "Go to the store and get me a lottery ticket. Everything that old woman said was true and we're about to be rich."

"You idiot," my uncle said. "We own a house and have two cars. You're already richer than that woman's wildest dreams."

That did put things into perspective.

Only about ten years later—after working their butts off, robbing Peter to pay Paul, and making some very smart decisions— my aunt and uncle were able to sell the small, wonderful retirement home they'd built from the ground up to a very large retirement chain for big bucks.

Theirs is a great American success story.

Memories And Memorials

On Memorial Day, Jack (my husband) and I received a text from our good friend Dave Bellon. Dave is a four-time combat veteran (two in Iraq, two in Afghanistan) and a Brigadier General in the United States Marine Corps. He and my husband go way back. As in back to sixth grade. And they have indulged in every kind of adolescent antic together—from sneaking whiskey and cigarettes on the railroad tracks, to jumping off Dave's roof and into his pool (beers in hand) while Dave's parents were out of town, to doing shameful things to girls who let them while they raged on spring break at some God-awful, dorm-like hotel in Daytona Beach.

Although we live several states apart, Dave and Jack still indulge in those meandering, soul-scrutinizing spaghetti bowl conversations that so many men quit having with their friends right around the time they graduate from college. For those men, sports take the place of a real exchange—one that risks exposure, intimacy. But not Jack and Dave. And that's what touches me so deeply about their friendship. Sure, they laugh, they needle each other, they tell dirty jokes, but their banter is the antithesis of small talk. In fact, they speak only of that which matters and it is as refreshing as a bath in the snow—Swedish style.

So that's why when my husband's iPhone pinged on

Memorial Day weekend and Dave's name came up, I knew he was reaching out.

It was a dreary Sunday in St. Louis, where Dave lives, and he was sitting in his suburban garage watching the rainstorm. And he was remembering friends who had fallen. Brave men he had come to think of as brothers before they were ripped from his life. He was thinking of two, in particular, and he asked that we share their names and their stories with our children. We did. And I'd like to share them here as well, if I may.

Lt. Col Kevin Shea (1966-2004)

Lt. Col. Kevin Shea was killed on September 14th, 2004 when he was mortally wounded in a rocket attack on Camp Fallujah in Al Anbar Province, Iraq. He was the highest ranking Marine to die in the Iraq War at the time of his death.

A 1984 graduate of Bishop O'Dea High School in Seattle, Washington, Shea accepted an appointment to the United States Air Force Academy, where he was a standout defensive end on the football team, played in the 1987 Freedom Bowl, and was a member of the academy's 1989 national champion rugby team.

After graduating, Shea accepted a commission as a 2nd lieutenant in the United States Marine Corps. There, he completed The Basic School (TBS) and the Infantry Officer's Course at Quantico, Virginia.

Shea's assignments included Support Company Detachment Commander, for the 9th Communications Battalion in Operation Desert Storm, Liaison Officer for Marine Forces Central Command (MARCENT) G-6, and JCSE Task Force Commander, Combined Special Operations Task Force, during Operation Desert Thunder, and Communications Officer (G-6) Regimental Combat

Team 1 (RCT-1), 1st Marine Division, Operation Iraqi Freedom II.

Shea also earned a Master of Science degree in electrical engineering at the Naval Postgraduate School in Monterey, California, and served as an instructor in electrical engineering and a rugby coach at the United States Naval Academy, where he was revered by the students.

Shea received the Bronze Star a few weeks before his death. He did not inform his family.

After his death, a highly anticipated rugby match between the Naval Academy, then ranked No. 3 in the nation, and its rival, the Air Force, was canceled when the Navy players decided unanimously to bow out to attend Shea's memorial and interment at Arlington.

The Marine Corps Scholarship Foundation administers a scholarship in Shea's name. There is a chapter about Shea in *In the Shadow of Greatness*, written by graduates of the Naval Academy.

The Kevin M. Shea Memorial Unit Award is given annually to a United States Marine Corps unit that makes exceptional contributions to the Corps.

Gy Sgt Mike Davis (1982-2001)

Gy Sgt. Mike Davis was killed on December 11, 2001 at only nineteen years of age. He is the son of Gy Sgt and Mrs. Michael L. Davis of the United States Marine Corps. His tombstone at the Barrancas National Cemetery in Pensacola, Florida, reads simply: *Gy Sgt USMC Gone Fishing*. For one so young, he left an indelible impression on all those who knew him, and the memory of his humor, his good nature, and his unflinching character goes some way to fill the hole vacated by his loss. And that's saying something.

Please pray for these men and their families. Share their names with your children. Don't let them be forgotten.

A Candle For Dina
A Prayer In Honor Of The Power Of Art

A number of years ago, I was agonizing over some of my own really bad prose in a cafe in San Francisco, when I overheard an older couple shooting the breeze in Czech at a table next to me.

As a Czech speaker myself, I really can't resist the urge to approach people who are conversing in my native tongue. Its harsh consonants and lilting vowels put a spell on me, and before I know it, I'm introducing myself and making off-color jokes.

That day was no exception.

Although the couple in question was still enjoying a pair of chocolate croissants and sipping espresso, I interrupted their breakfast and chatted them up long enough to meet their son, whom they were visiting from Britain. By the end of our little coffee klatch, we had exchanged contact information and I'd invited them to come to our apartment for an authentic Czech meal of duck, sweet and sour cabbage, and dumplings.

They did, and we had a marvelous time.

As an added bonus, their son, a psychiatrist, painter, M.D., lover of opera and wearer of costumes on any given day just for the fun of it, went on to become a friend. Our acquaintance with this true British eccentric, along with great memories of good times had, also provided us with a unique opportunity to meet an extraordinary woman.

You see, our friend's aunt, Dina Babbitt, was—and I don't know how else to describe it—"famous" in holocaust circles. As a young art student, Dina, along with her mother, was deported first to Terezin, then Auschwitz. A lot of Czech Jews traveled this route during World War II. They would initially spend some months in the Nazi "showcase" camp featured in the German propaganda film *Hitler Gives the Jews a Town*, and they would then be transferred to camps that had dropped the pretense of acting like anything other than death factories.

Ironically, it was Dina's expulsion from the less barbarous Terezin that would save both hers and her mother's life.

Once installed in the section of Auschwitz called Birkenau, where most of the inmates were interned, Dina was asked by a friend to help make the family camp appear less depressing. It was for the children's sake more than the adults'—a way to buffer some of the harsh realities around them and allow a few simple moments of joy and play into their lives.

Her efforts did more than that.

A gifted painter, Dina recreated a scene from the Disney classic *Snow White* on the cheerless walls, providing the children with glimpses of their favorite fairy tale and giving their parents a reminder of their own God-given humanity. Perhaps even offering some hope. A smile, after all, is an expression of hope, and you couldn't help but to smile at the sight of Dina's mural.

The inmates, of course, were not the only ones watching.

Dina's images caught the attention of Dr. Joseph Mengele—Auschwitz's Angel of Death, as he was called. Mengele had begun medical experiments on, at that time, mostly gypsy inmates and was dissatisfied with photographs he'd had taken of his victims. He would later complain to Dina that photography was for peasants and could never be considered a real art form.

But he had much higher esteem for Dina's talents and ordered her to come to his infirmary to draw and paint his macabre handy-work.

Dina agreed, but only on one condition. She told him that she would kill herself in the electric fence surrounding the camp if he didn't save her mother's life as well.

Mengele narrowed his eyes and grinned. "What's her number?" he said.

Dina told me this story and many others on the day I got to spend with her at her rustic home in Bonny Doon, near the Santa Cruz mountains. She lived deep in the woods because even after all this time, she was still afraid that Mengele could hunt her down and kill her because she'd known him so well and could identify him. After the war, he had fled to Argentina and never been captured.

"It's nonsense," she said. "He'd be over a hundred years old by now, but I can't put my fear to death."

It was an interesting choice of words.

"So, why did you invite a stranger like me to your house?" I asked her. I had been told how wary she was not only of Mengele, but of people she didn't know.

"I wanted to speak Czech, of course!" she told me with a wink.

And she did, to my great pleasure, tell me story after story in her elegant Czech throughout much of the day.

"I could never have survived without my mother, nor she without me," Dina said.

She went on to explain how she and her mother had lived through a death march together. Dina, sick with dysentery, was trying to hide her condition from Nazi guards who would shoot anyone who was too tired or ill to continue. Anyone with visible signs of disease. In a moment both comic and tragic, Dina's mother slinked out of her underwear in a sexy way and handed them to her daughter so that she could wipe the diarrhea off her legs. "Happy birthday," her mother said, and the two of them burst into fits of laughter right there during the march. That, in and of itself, nearly got them killed.

She also reminisced about her marriage to Art Babbitt, whom she had met in Paris after the war, when she was interviewing to work as an animator for Warner Brothers. Babbitt, in one of those remarkable coincidences that somehow seem commonplace in wartime, had been an animator on Disney's *Snow White* and the inspiration for the mural that would spare Dina's life.

They married shortly after and went on to live what Dina described as a "very Hollywood" sort of life. She rolled her eyes when she said it, telling me about the end of their marriage as well.

"He had a woman," she said. "And I discovered this. 'She means nothing to me!' He told me over and over again."

I was struck at how there wasn't a trace of self-pity in her voice as Dina recounted her husband's betrayal.

"What a stupid thing to say," she went on. "I told him, 'If you had said—I'm sorry, Dina, my heart took me to her. I couldn't stop myself. I love her—then maybe then I could have forgiven you. But you dishonored our marriage for someone who meant nothing to you? A passing pleasure? Tell me, I said to him. If they come for me again, will you show them where I'm hiding because our marriage means so little to you that you would risk it for a girl who means nothing?"

Dina left her husband and their glamorous life without looking back.

There was, however, one thing that Dina could not stop looking back on. In the early 1970s, she became aware that several of her paintings of Mengele's medical experiments were still in existence. They had been confiscated by the Polish government after the war and were to be used as part of a permanent installation at the Auschwitz-Birkenau museum complex.

She was invited to view them, and, she thought, take them with her back to her home in California. But the Polish government had other plans. The paintings were part of Poland's national historical heritage, they told her. Incredibly, they also explained to her at one point that if anyone had any real claim to the paintings, it would be Mengele's heirs.

Dina would not stop fighting for her right to her paintings. They had been created with her soul's blood in exchange for her mother's life. Their subjects' eyes would haunt her dreams until the day she died.

But despite the help of numerous Jewish groups, national and international publications, illustrious intermediaries, and even the American government, it was not meant to be.

Dina Babbitt, survivor of Auschwitz and death marches, reluctant chronicler of the Angel of Death, died of cancer in 2009 without her paintings in her possession.

Tonight, in honor of you, Dina, in honor of how art can save lives and inspire hope under even the most dire circumstances, in reverence to my and my husband's one quarter heritage, we'll light a candle and say a prayer on this first night of Hanukkah.

[served cold]

James Brown Is In My Hot Tub

We have a thing for James Brown in our household, and I want to give the man a nod today because he's dispensed so much joy to me and my family over the years. Like a screaming, dancing, cackling, "hey"-ing Pez container.

He's made us sing, he's made us shake our booties in a way white people don't often do, and he's made us laugh. Okay, I admit, we are kind of laughing at him sometimes. But it's a laugh that comes from a good place—like the way I crack up when I make fun of my mother's accent.

And that's really what it comes down to with James and my clan. Because, yes, we love his music. Our children were potty-trained to "Hot Pants." But what it's really about is that James Brown feels like a member of our family—my side of it, that is.

Like my crazy Czech family, he's a gaudy dresser—glittering, brassy, ostentatious. Just Google a mid-nineteen eighties picture of James with Janet and Michael Jackson and the Rev. Al Sharpton. He makes them look like country club Republicans.

Which brings me to my next point. James was a great fan of Richard Nixon.

If you've read some of the previous essays in this volume, you probably know that President Nixon is to my parents what a Terrence Malick film is to most film aficionados. Deeply misunderstood by the masses.

James's Republican activism was sort of ignored in the recent biopic about the Godfather of Soul, *Get On Up*, and it's a damned shame. James Brown was an American original, not some pretender who showed up at all the right events just to get a pat on the back. He loved Nixon and he loved Al Sharpton. That wasn't a contradiction in his mind. And his mind wasn't for sale. He loved Ronald Reagan and he loved Ray Charles. He truly loved black America.

There was nothing you could say or do that was going to get him to back-peddle on that. Or even try to make sense of it for you.

He had a kind of empirical purity that, to me, is the very definition of soul. Our souls, after all, are what make us unique, human, eternal. James Brown wasn't going to bargain his soul away for anything.

In a world where everyone's trying so hard to be loved by everybody, and is always going to great pains to say the right thing, isn't that refreshing?

Of course his personal life was a technicolor mess. He enjoyed good liquor and bad drugs. He had a weakness for nasty women. The kind of gals who aren't there when you wake up in the morning (or afternoon) and neither is your wallet. Sometimes he tied them up and wouldn't let them leave. He rarely checked the birth dates on their IDs.

But he remained close to his first wife, Velma, until the day he died. He loved her.

When I think about other musicians whose work has moved me, been a part of the fabric of my life, I often have to make a conscious effort to chase the images from their personal foibles from my mind. The Mamas and the Papas come to mind, Janis Joplin, Michael Jackson, obviously.

But somehow with James Brown, I don't mind his mug shots. I can take his life and his music as a whole without cringing or wanting to cry at certain parts. I can even look at the end of his life that way, despite the fact that he essentially died of self-abuse.

Maybe it's the unbridled exuberance in his voice as it blares from my iPod. He had a runaway thirst for life that's present in only a handful of public figures. Maybe it's just because he was always gloriously and authentically James Brown—even at his worst.

Hard-Boiled Thrillers, Noir, And The Belly Laugh

Recently, I started a discussion on Crimespace (a crime/thriller uber-fan sight I highly recommend for those obsessed with city lights, cigarettes, bad women, and rye whiskey). I posed this question: Is there a place for humor in a hard-boiled thriller/noir? The answers I got were mixed, but there was a hesitancy that trended towards "No." One Crimespacer quoted Otto Penzler—"Noir requires a sense of bleakness and despair, and characters so flawed, their failure is in their DNA."

Maybe I'm too much of a black-humor-Eastern European-type gal, but isn't that level of failure—the kind at the cellular level—kind of funny in and of itself? Raymond Chandler was a master of this kind of humor. His characters were funny—they were wry, off-kilter, even pathetic. A conspicuous longing punctuated their wisecracks instead of the usual punch line; he used the screech of a tire in place of a pa-dum-pum. I mean really, is there a better comic line than, "From thirty feet away she looked like a lot of class. From ten feet away she looked like something made up to be seen from thirty feet away." Taken out of context, that's a line that could have just as easily come out of *Saturday Night Live*.

We've all become very serious since Chandler, I think.

Sure, we enjoy our comic thrillers like *Skin Deep* from Carl Hiaasen, but ultimately, when talking about thrillers in and of themselves—what we call real thrillers, we take on the oh, so serious tone of John la Carre, who writes great books, and is not a funny guy. In fact, as good as he is you've got to admit that he often takes on the moralizing tone of an old-fashioned Catholic school principal. Sometimes, when I'm curled up with one of his books and having one of my black humor thoughts, I can almost hear him say, "That's not funny, young lady."

But Sam Spade is funny. He looks at the world through a piece of warped glass and laughs at how you can look short and fat when he tips it this way, and noodle-skinny when he tips it that. He might even tell you so before he pops you one. And Raymond Chandler seems like the guy you want sitting next to you on a bar stool. You'd sit there all night if you could, pretending you've got no place else to go, just to listen to his take on life.

Maybe we've forgotten how some of the funniest people in our own lives are the ones who've had the hardest knocks. And maybe those people ought to start making their way back into our thrillers—no matter what's at stake. Whether it's just a two-bit heist or the whole damn world.

Bill Withers Is Still The Bomb

A couple of weeks ago, my husband and I watched a BBC documentary on 1970s R&B singer-songwriter Bill Withers.

And it was nothing like what I expected.

Little of his incredible music was featured—which is strange considering his long list of hits, including "Lean on Me," "Ain't No Sunshine," "Grandma's Hands," "Just the Two of Us," and an impressive list of lesser known, beautifully written songs that hit the tops of the R&B charts. Music that confounded the record industry because it didn't focus on the usual trinity of romantic love, sex and dance to seduce an audience.

Bill Withers's songs were more often about friendship, grief, or an old lady he adored. But the pop-loving, disco-dancing public embraced them anyway.

"You have no idea how good you are," he was told by one producer.

But the documentary focused on the man, not the art, and I found myself utterly moved.

Now, "moved" is not a word I most often associate with musicians and other celebrities. I'm not a fame junkie and I don't think I've ever in my life been interested in obtaining an autograph from anyone living or dead.

But if there is one artist I'd like to share a coffee with on my porch, it would be Bill Withers.

Not because I love his music—although I do. I can just call up his music on the iPod, though, you know? It's not because of his rural, hard-scrabble childhood in West Virginia—even if I do have a thing for West Virginia. Or the fact that he rose above a significant stuttering problem and the racism of his era. Those are all great things, mind you, but lots of successful people have had to overcome massive obstacles. Ones that make it hard for some folks just to get out of bed in the morning, let alone rise to the top of a hugely competitive profession.

What most impressed me about Bill Withers was his quiet demeanor. Here was a nuanced, unassuming man who wasn't pretending to be humble—he wasn't pretending anything. He just was what he was—a human being with soul-freeing talent that doesn't come at you, but takes you into its arms.

As we sat glued to the screen, my husband and I saw no star sitting Zen-like in his overly engineered life, spewing talking points about his commitment to the environment, or the rain forest, or other worthy causes his people have briefed him on. Causes that are actually being addressed hands-on by scientists, missionaries, companies, and non-profits. Bill Withers doesn't seem to go for that BS, but he doesn't judge it either, or sit above it.

Bill Withers just sits in his comfortable but homey house in California, watching TV and hanging out with his friends or his pretty wife and family. The only extravagances visible are the occasional Jacob Lawrence painting, which you'd swear was just a framed print given the unassuming nature of the house that surrounds it. And there's a music studio, too, where Withers and his lovely daughter make music together.

When he hears her sing, he cries.

Want To Understand Marriage?
Watch *Naked and Afraid* On Discovery Channel

Unlike "distraction TV," which simply takes you out of your life for a while—the day-to-day grind of ditching the secret police, escaping the clutches of a sadistic assassin, making love to a charismatic Russian diplomat... oh, wait, no, that's the book I'm writing.

(insert snippets from your daily grind here)

Anyway, my point is, Discovery Channel's *Naked and Afraid* actually teaches you something. It is, in my opinion, the best microcosm for marriage you can find on the small screen—or anywhere else for that matter.

Before I get into that, I want to start with a bit of marriage advice that my Aunt Viki gave me when I was still a teenager. It was great advice and I've never forgotten it. I thought hard on it before I even met my husband, and I'm so glad I did.

She said (translated from the Czech language), "First of all, never marry someone who's weaker than you. You might think you're going to be okay with it, and a more delicate mate might even make you feel good at the outset. You might feel needed and safe as a result. Strong. But don't be fooled. First of all, no matter how much your little flower might seem to need or worship you, weaklings are the first to jump ship when the going gets rough. And even if they stay, in the long run, you'll lose respect for them, and a marriage can't survive that."

Amen, sister.

"And whatever you do," she continued. "Make sure the mate you choose is someone you want to come home to whether you're living in a one room flat or a ten-bedroom mansion. Someone you truly enjoy talking to and laughing with. You don't know how quickly fortunes can change or what life has in store for you and I've seen a lot of marriages crumble when the money disappears and they have to live a simpler life. But I've seen just as many fall apart when things turn for the better."

She also said that it's important to like how your mate smells, but that's neither here nor there in this post (although I wholeheartedly agree).

Truer words have probably been spoken, but hers are pretty darned good. And there are few shows that put my aunt's wisdom on display better than *Naked and Afraid*.

If you're not familiar with the concept, let me enlighten you: Two strangers—a man and a woman who both claim some level of survival skills— are dropped naked and presumably afraid (or at the very least apprehensive) into a hostile, natural environment such as the Amazon, the desert, or the tundra. They're allowed to take one tool with them each (most choose a fire starter or a knife of some sort) and that's it. No phone. No lights. No motorcars. Not a single luxury.

They must survive for twenty-one days—hunting and gathering their food, keeping their fire burning, dealing with stinging and biting insects (think naked here), snakes, wild boars, torrential downpours, blistering days, freezing nights (again—naked) and most importantly—each other.

We've all observed various couple dynamics in our own

lives: The husband and wife who bicker incessantly, yet march on to make an illogically successful life together, the lovers whose passion starts out so hot but fizzles when they actually have to leave the bedroom and do everyday things like shop for groceries or visit the DMV, the passive-aggressive couple who can never be happy for each other's successes, yet resent each other's failures with equal determination, the pair who does their own thing, living separate but equal lives, the partners in a lifelong love affair that takes your breath away as they walk hand-in-hand through triumph and travail.

Not only are all of these pairings and more glimpsed on *Naked and Afraid*'s scant hour, but you are taken through a condensed version of a particular brand of marriage from start to finish in the course of that time. Some make it, but barely, others bail out altogether and end up going home before the first week is up. A few just rock it and leave you feeling energized and invigorated.

I should tell you at this point that I watch *Naked and Afraid* almost exclusively with my nearly thirteen-year-old son. It offers us that rare combination of experience where we can enjoy something low-brow and seventh-grade-boy together, while still not missing out on my being able to impart a genuine life lesson that isn't coming straight from me, and allows my kid to draw his own conclusions.

My kid: "I can't believe she wasted all that time making a pentagram out of vines while he was out hunting for food!"

Me: "Yeah, well, you know, she's into Wicca and that. She did it to ward off bad luck or something."

My kid: "That's fine, but you do that when you've already got a fire started and you've found a water source."

Me: "Hmmm."

My kid: "I bet her real-life husband made her come on this show. I bet she acts like that at home and makes him do everything while she just farts around."

Then we make our bets.

My kid: They both bail, but she goes first.

Me: They both bail, but he's outta there.

I won that round.

My kid: "I liked that couple where he was a military guy and she was like a nature-type hippie person."

I nod. I liked them, too. Both had made it through the *Naked and Afraid* gauntlet with other partners and were put together when a really annoying pair of vain whiners bailed out.

My kid: "You know what was cool about them? They each had things they knew how to do and brought those to the situation, and when things went wrong they never blamed stuff on each other—even if it really was one of their faults. They just moved on and made the best of it."

Me: "I loved how they high-fived each other at the end."

My kid: "That was awesome."

This is where my Aunt Viki's marriage speech really dove tails with the inherent genius of *Naked and Afraid*. You see, like many people in my family, my aunt knows a thing or two about surviving hardship. With her husband of over forty years, she's been through every scenario she described and then some.

And in her wisdom, what she was really saying was as daunting as it is true.

When choosing a mate, you not only have to feel that indescribable something that draws you to a person in the first place. That makes you want to kiss their face every morning, make their coffee, go to their office Christmas party, listen to their music, and cuddle with them even when they're kind of clammy and gross.

You also have to know in your heart that if there was an apocalypse—zombies, nuclear war, an alien invasion—the two of you could at least have a shot in hell at making it through alive.

A Seven Year-Old's Thoughts
On Michael Jackson, Before And After "Thriller"

My youngest daughter was perched at my husband's computer the other day, while I sat opposite her in an armchair sorting through bills.

She was watching an early video of Michael Jackson's—"Blame It on the Boogie"—and I couldn't help but notice her face. Her eyes were wide and focused, her lips in an open-mouthed smile.

She was beaming.

Her delight was contagious, so I decided to live a little. I dumped my mail into a pile at my feet and went to sit beside her. We watched "Blame It on the Boogie" three times, then "Don't Stop 'Til You Get Enough" and "Rock With You." Over and over. I showed her "Beat It" and "Thriller," then "Billie Jean," but it was when we moved past the "Thriller" album—onto "HIStory," "Bad" and "Dangerous"—that her interest waned. Not entirely, but it was clear her attention had gone from rapturous to merely entertained. She'd lost that look of unbridled joy that had drawn me to her side in the first place.

And I'd lost it, too, even if I was still a little hungry for the shot of bliss Jackson's early videos had given me. It was the pop culture equivalent of a hangover—the kind of bluesy, reflective state that washes over you after watching

Judy Garland in the "Wizard of Oz" and thinking *what the hell happened?*

In "Boogie" there's a sense of wonder. Jackson moved with an easy grace and basked in his performance. There was a give and take with the audience that flowed like a perfect kiss. All sweet and tender but on fire at the same time.

His dancing was raw, almost childlike. And although he was on stage with his talented brothers, he was the only one you wanted to watch. As I sat writing this post, I had to call it back up on my screen, then get up and dance. I couldn't help myself.

Fast forward to "Bad," which was good, but forced, over-choreographed, and detached. Jackson had wind machines blowing at him and sported a quasi-military outfit that jingled like a charm bracelet. His face, so handsome, had already begun its transformation—looking chiseled and waxy.

Everything about him seemed to say "go away."

My daughter's interest was piqued again when I showed her pictures of Jackson's metamorphosis. Yet I found myself at a loss when it came to explaining to her why it happened. To talk about childhood trauma, or the trappings of fame, or the loneliness that some very talented people feel seemed trite. I didn't know Michael Jackson, after all, and it felt silly to try and psychoanalyze him.

But as usual, she bested me.

"Frankenstein," she said. She was looking at a picture of Jackson at his worst—towards the end of his life.

Frankenstein is a big theme for her. She loves the original 1933 black and white film as much as the 1974 Mel Brooks parody.

I've always thought it's because she, herself, has so many scars—from the many surgeries she had to endure at birth, to the fact that no one could hold her until she was several weeks old and could actually tolerate the pain of being moved and cuddled. Whatever the case, she feels a kinship with Mary Shelley's dark protagonist, and was able to make the connection between the fictional character and the very real Michael Jackson.

And as I looked at the pictures of Jackson that spanned from his youth in the Jackson 5 to his beyond the stratosphere fame, I felt the urge to hunt down a quote from Mary Shelley's classic horror novel—one that I could only remember in vague terms, but I knew it would fit.

"I was dependent on none and related to none. The path of my departure was free, and there was none to lament my annihilation. My person was hideous and my stature gigantic. What did this mean? Who was I? What was I? Whence did I come? What was my destination? These questions continually recurred, but I was unable to solve them."—the Monster.

Dracula: The Gothic Pimp

Despite my almost unnatural love for the thriller—especially the spy thriller—my favorite novel of all time is actually Bram Stoker's *Dracula*. It is, in my humble opinion, the most highly original and genuinely terrifying story I have ever read. Bram Stoker has brought into the public consciousness a character so confounding, erudite, and manly in the classical sense, that I think it's safe to say that he's the only monster that makes women want to both scream and swoon.

The whole vampire genre has given new meaning to the Bible's warning to resist "the glamor of evil." It has turned us into undead junkies and actually convinced us that becoming a murdering, blood-sucking, night-dwelling, hell-bound, semi-immortal creature might not be so bad. Not if we get to spend much of that time cozying up to the count in his coffin.

And while Frank Langella was probably the first to interpret our favorite vampire (no, not Edward) in a blatantly romantic way, the raw material was always there.

Dracula looks a woman straight in the eyes and stares blatantly, lustfully at her body. He runs his lips softly over the skin of her neck. His whispers his needs into her ear. Salacious moves aside, his manners are courtly and well, perfect. According to legend, he can't even enter your house unless you invite him in.

He's a pretty good dresser, too, in an old fashioned sort of way. And can he dance? You bet! No white man's overbite there.

But I think what makes Dracula such a fine ladies' man in spite of his obvious limitations—namely, being a demon from hell who wants to drain you of all of your blood—is something many of us women are loathe to admit. It's what makes the modern man—schooled in the art of sensitive conduct—want to slam his fist into a table and scream "Unfair!" and makes liberated women from all over seethe with righteous anger.

It's that like it or not, when Dracula unbuttons the top button of our lacy nightgown and says in that deep, commanding voice of his, "You will cross land or sea to do my bidding," even the most strident of us want to whisper, "Okay."

This is the menace not of love, but desire.

Dracula reminds us in the most primal way that passion is by its very nature inequitable. Sexual cravings in their purest sense are about power—the gain and the loss of it. Sex is unreasonable, apolitical and utterly uninterested in cultural trends. It is objectifying. From the curve of a face, to the taste of a pair of lips. The glimpse of an expensive watch on a man's wrist or the view of a ripe pair of breasts bursting out of a white blouse. Even a succulent vein pulsing with hot, crimson blood.

And what makes Count Dracula such an insidious figure is not that a woman doesn't know he's a monster—that he's pulled one over on her somehow. From the first time she catches his sly glance, she knows exactly what he's about. Just as a woman knows when a certain man will never call her again, no matter how thunderously the earth moved as their bodies came together.

For no amount of scholarship, activism, jargon or indignation is likely to change the nature of desire.

As long as we are human, no matter how enlightened we may become, I suspect sex will always be there to lead us so far astray that we will give up anything—including our hard-earned independence, our rights, our very souls—for the briefest taste of its magic.

Jan Saudek: The Straight Robert Mapplethorpe

I want to devote this week to one of my favorite artists: the Czech photographer Jan Saudek.

Let me give you a quick course that'll at least make you fluent in cocktail party parlance. Saudek is a Czech photographer whose quasi-surreal, often erotic, and always drop-jaw stunning pictures have been making the rounds since the 1950s. Saudek himself is half Jewish and spent part of his youth in the Terezin concentration camp in Czechoslovakia. Maybe that's where he discovered that the beautiful and the grotesque are inextricably linked—much like pleasure and pain. Saudek is able to elevate the monstrous, the bizarre, the kinky, the ludicrous, into things of allure that delight the senses instead of making us cringe.

Sexuality is a big theme for Saudek, and he depicts sex with an abandon that frankly, makes me blush. For Saudek, sex can be coy, worshipful, wanton, and depraved all at once. You walk away knowing only one thing—he likes it. A lot. And he makes you like it, too, and in ways you never thought possible.

Quirky, kinky, raw, deeply sentimental, Saudek is a true Slav—one who celebrates his contrary nature and is able to elevate the most hideous scene—a topless, heavily made-up woman with a gun in her mouth, or enormous bare and dimpled buttocks smiling defiantly, alluringly at the camera - into a thing of beauty. I call him the straight Robert Mapplethorpe, and if you take a look at some of his photos, you'll understand why. Saudek, like Mapplethorpe, is one kinky bastard and has no compunction about putting himself—in all his glory—in front of the camera. He allows us to see him in most any manner of sexually deviant or merely sexual contexts—spanking, giving and receiving oral sex, making love to obese women, naked, in shackles. He gives Christian Grey a run for his money.

But Saudek is also unflinching in his ability to depict a simple act of love—something so sentimental that it could be the cover to a romance novel. A lot of artists are more than happy to showcase sex, violence, depravity, pain, and yet cannot train their eye on love. That's too much exposure—perhaps they think it's anti-intellectual. Yet Jan Saudek will photograph babies from the same adoring, kitten-love vantage as Anne Geddes—only without the kitsch. He forces us to take our most sloppy, gushy emotions as seriously as we often take ourselves. In the serious art world, that's a hell of a lot more brave than political advocacy or some raunchy pictures. It's downright radical.

And isn't that what art is supposed to be about?

The Lost Art Of The Bad Family Photo

I love family photos. Or any kind of personal Kodak moment—the bonz-ai! college party, the first dance, the accidental nudie.

And I don't just love my family photos. I love yours, too. I love my neighbor's from down the street, I love my worst enemy's family photos—especially if I get my hands on them.

Family photographs are the first thing I look for when I'm invited into someone's home. Books are second, but that's another story.

I can tell usually within a few minutes of looking around if this is a second family, for instance. One that was torn apart by divorce and then painstakingly recreated. If it's a close family. If I want these people in my life as more than acquaintances.

It's the voyeur in me, you could say—certainly. But it's not a *National Enquirer*-style prurient voyeurism, not the bad beach body kind.

To me, personal photographs are as much a window into someone's soul as their eyes are. And there's no better place to get a look at the snapshots of a human being's life than in their own home. The iPhone montage just doesn't do it for me. Nor does the Facebook collection.

I must see the photographs within their native habitat, on their own cultural ground. Whether in an immaculate living room befitting a *Southern Living* feature spread, or cluttering an already tchotchke-jammed consul in a den populated with worn, comfy armchairs—the kind of armchairs that if they were people, would be doughy around the middle and dozing off after a meat and potatoes orgy.

More than coffeehouse chatter, or Facebook friendship, and certainly more than a resume, uncensored family photographs telegraph who we are in a way that is becoming increasingly rare in our controlled lives, where each us has become his own PR machine.

With Photoshop and all the new fancy-schmancy cameras out there that make everyone a potential professional photographer, I feel like our bad family photos are getting lost. Replaced by an image-conscious collage of freeze-frames designed to make our lives look like one big *Friends* episode.

As much as social media has put our lives on display (sometimes in a cringe-making way), the delete button has made it oh-so easy to erase every cock-eyed, true dork, zit-faced, fashion-don't candid that's ever been taken of us. We used to have to hunt those photographs down and actually burn them out of existence.

Most of the time, they just got stuffed into the back of a photo album—only to be trotted out at a rehearsal dinner or a 40th birthday, or worse, flaunted by an evil sibling the first time you bring someone you really like home. That person you want desperately to see you as the cool cat you've become. But maybe, who you discover—as they're gaping at that picture of you in plaid pants and a bad perm—will like you even more for the nerd you were and perhaps still are on the inside.

[don't laugh]

Life In A Haunted House

We never get any trick-or-treaters. I can tell myself that it's because we're the only house on a dead-end street and surely, being off the beaten path is part of the problem. But if I'm to be completely honest, it's because I know that little kids are afraid of our home.

Yes, we live in *that* house.

It's the one we all dared each other to visit on Halloween. The one that got the occasional egging from only the bravest, most rebellious teens. The one that made toddlers cry.

In the neighborhood I grew up in outside of Chicago, there was a dark, recessed house that looked like a Turkish prison. It definitely stuck out, as the rest of the homes in our neighborhood had been built in the early 1960s and had a decidedly family-friendly feel to them. Swing sets in the back yard, goofy Halloween decorations and middle class tastes made them look safe, even when the masters of those homes appeared grumpy and mean, and the mistresses depressed, lonely and on the edge.

At the Turkish prison house, my friend Laura and I would get about as far as ringing the doorbell, but ultimately, we'd chicken out and run away. I don't think we ever got candy from those people, and if we had, we would've probably stuffed it in their mailbox before high-tailing it out of there. We were afraid that any loot we might've scored was laced with arsenic, battery acid, or just plain old bad juju.

I recognize now that the unfortunate, in all likelihood sweet-as-heck folks who lived in that house waited in vain every Halloween for someone—anyone—to come by and put a dent in that bag of Hershey's Minis they felt obligated to buy every year . . . just in case.

I know that's what we do.

Maybe you're thinking, "Aw, come on. It can't be that bad. You seem nice enough—I'm sure there's a very good reason why no one will trick-or-treat at your house."

And there is.

Our house is haunted.

It's no surprise, as our house is really, really old and has had a lot of traffic. She was built while Thomas Jefferson was still among us and living across town for heaven's sake, cross-breeding heirloom vegetables and writing letters that now sit in the Smithsonian. She's been a general store, grain depot, bar, theater, voting place, boarding house, student ghetto, and a musician's flophouse (we've been told Art Garfunkel partied at our home in the 1960s—scary, right?), until finally, over the course of two owners, she morphed into a single-family home.

I think our basement is the crux of the problem. An old-fashioned wet basement, it looks like something out of an Indiana Jones movie. It is populated by numerous snakes and spiders that we welcome as part of the delicate ecosystem of our house, as those critters keep the mouse and insect population in check. But that's not why I mention it, and it's not why little kids who don't know us do the fifty-yard dash past our property line.

It's that our basement was also once used as a (gulp!) Civil War morgue.

So maybe that's where all of the cling-clangs, footsteps, apparitions and ghostly murmurs come from!

Case in point, in our most recent paranormal encounter, I got up in the middle of the night to fetch myself some water. When I returned to our bed, I distinctly heard a man's whisper and turned to my husband.

"Did you say something, honey?" I said.

My husband told me that he had not.

"But I heard it, too," he said. "Let's talk about it in the morning." Which we did, but without the drama and hullabaloo you might imagine.

We're not afraid anymore. We've been living here long enough to know that these odd occurrences are just our home's way of saying hello every once in a while.

And that's what I'm getting at.

As spooky as our house may seem to outsiders, we know she loves and protects us.

Like a loyal, old crone, she objects loudly and emphatically to people who annoy, interfere or in any way attempt to cause mischief in our lives.

When my grandmother got ornery and meddling in the years before she died, our house would actually respond to her visits—keeping her up at night with grating, intermittent noises that tormented my Baba's sleep like Chinese water-torture. The plumbing wouldn't behave for her, temperature controls would go haywire and the guest room TV screen might simply go on strike.

I don't have to tell you that all of these petty annoyances would vanish the moment Baba pulled out of our driveway, Rush Limbaugh blasting from her radio and a cloud of cigarette smoke billowing out of the passenger side window.

Now, I loved my grandmother—even at her worst. But my house? Not so much. She always preferred the company of my more cheerful mom, who accompanied my grandmother on her visits, but would remain curiously unbothered by the woo-woo goings on.

And I love that our house is strong—clad in history's armor. Thick-walled and made of brick. She barely shakes when the trains go by, standing broad-chested and chivalrous; a black, Southern grandmother. She has been a friend and safe haven throughout violent weather, illness and economic catastrophe. Even when we've scowled at her and bristled at the tyranny of caring for her scratches, bruises, and idiosyncrasies.

But we have never let her down either, and she knows it.

My husband and I have fought her and fought for her, fixing her face-paint, finding the right doctors for her Edison-era wiring, buying her a brand new roof that sits on her head like a Sunday hat. No more piles of cold, young men, whooping cowboys, tired merchants, transients, or naked hippies. Our children have filled her life with laughter. They've hidden their secrets in her many nooks and crannies and papered her walls with their dreams.

We have given her a happy family.

So, please, consider coming by this Halloween. We have all the good kinds of candy, and you're sure to get a big handful instead of the usual one piece allotment that more popular homes dispense.

The Santa Quandary

This will undoubtedly be my ten-year-old daughter's last year as a believer in the fat man in red. She's already informed me that apart from her usual letter to Santa, she's written him a secret letter, just in case her friends at school are right and Santa is, in fact, a big sham perpetrated by her parents.

"You think Santa doesn't know what you're up to?" I asked her.

But she wasn't buying it.

Already, she's decided that the Tooth Fairy is bogus, the Easter Bunny is "SO obviously" her mom and dad, and don't even get her started on leprechauns and St. Patrick's Day. This one I actually made up. Not the leprechauns part, of course, but the fact that chocolates fall out of leprechaun's pockets as they scamper around the yard early morning on St. Paddy's Day. Don't ask me why I invented yet another fictional creature that I now have to masquerade as—dropping chocolates all over our grass at some ungodly hour every year on March 17th—but there you have it.

I have to be honest, at this point I'm not really all that sad to see Santa go.

I'm ready. Even if I have a seven-year-old who, technically, still believes. After my son, the oldest, stopped believing, I could feel the whole Santa thing losing steam in our house. Like a pinhole in a balloon. I think we only kept up the ruse because the above-mentioned middle child has always been an ardent believer in magic. While she hates church and has expressed skepticism and sometimes downright hostility to our Catholic faith, large bunny rabbits who hide eggs and fill baskets with chocolate, portly saints in Finnish snow suits, and tiny, red-bearded men in green have never bothered her.

And now that she's getting ready to make the jump from magic to realism, there isn't much there that's there anymore, if you know what I mean? Especially since our youngest child has only a passing interest in Santa Claus.

She doesn't care who delivers her presents as long as she gets some.

I know a lot of parents see this transition as a huge loss. I'm sure I'll be one of them down the line. The Santa years have been magical. I've loved hiding my kids' presents at a neighbor's house, then waiting up until midnight on Christmas Eve to trudge over there and retrieve them. I've loved the unbridled delight on my children's faces Christmas morning, the half-eaten cookies and footprints around the tree. One year a family of deer must have tramped through our yard and their hoof prints in the light snow became a holy site for our son. At least until the fifty-degree weather melted them away.

When our kids were really little—as in, they'd swallow any fib we could concoct—we went so far as to convince our two eldest that they'd taken a ride on the Polar Express. My husband printed two golden tickets off of his computer and we tucked them into our children's pajama pockets, stamped with the words "believe."

But I'm ready to make the transition from Santa Claus, aka, it's all about me, to Christ and the spirit of what

Christmas is all about. I'm ready to start asking my children to give, and they're ready, too. I can see it in how short their lists have become, compared to other years. I hear the change in the way prayers are said before meal time and bed. The intercessory prayers that used to be a staple—*please, God, help me guess how many jellybeans are in the jar so that I can win that gift certificate to GameStop*—have begun to fade away. Instead, their conversations with God have become increasingly peppered with moments of gratitude—*thank you for the love in my life, and for the Dairy Queen Blizzard mom bought us after our cross country meet. Thank you for a home.*

It is a glorious transformation—like watching the sun rise. Even our little agnostic has taken up the cause.

In that spirit, I'd like to say thank you, God, for blessing me beyond reason with love, purpose, and a sense of meaning. A life without those things is sterile and literal. Rational to the point of aimlessness.

And thank you for helping me believe. I know it hasn't been easy.

New Year's Wisdom
From President Richard M. Nixon (Don't Laugh)

Everyone has a string of bad luck from time to time. The raw deal years roll over and over your toes like the grooved tires of a loaded pick-up truck. The boon years feel like one glass of champagne after another, but without the succeeding headache and the pictures of you doing handstands wearing only underwear . . . or less.

For us, the bum luck began shortly after the New Year in 2007 and ran until 2011 or 2012. When I look back on pictures of us from that time, my husband and I appear easily ten years older than we do now.

It started with a diagnosis. Our baby was going to be born with a tumor. Then, like a bad party, things just kept getting worse and no one would give us a ride home. Our baby was premature, the tumor turned out to be cancerous, the cancer needed to be treated, surgeries ensued, and then came the interminable waiting. Waiting to see if the cancer would come back, if our little girl would be normal—whatever that means, and waiting to see how we would emerge from this as a family. In the middle of all of this waiting, the economy crashed, forcing us to wait some more. Wait and see if our business would survive, if it could recover, if we had the smarts and the gumption to adapt.

Waiting not just to see if we could pull through—we did—but thrive again. We did that, too. Thank God.

There were a lot of things that got us through those years. Love, for one. We've been blessed with a lot of it. A backbone—both my husband and I were raised by no-nonsense people whose eyes glaze over the moment a self-pitying cadence enters any given conversation. Friends, family, and even downright strangers prayed for us, lent an ear, offered advice, or just offered to hold our hands.

One of those people was former President Richard Nixon.

"The finest steel has to go through the hottest fire," he said.

I've collected quotes since I was a little girl. My husband is downright obsessed with them. And not just the inspirational ones. Funny, brainy, polarizing, dark, and downright insane bits of speech all work their way onto our family quote board, which is presided over by my husband in his home office.

We like all kinds of quotes and they don't have to be from people we particularly admire. They just have to mean something to us—ring a bell at a poignant time in our lives. Speaking for myself, I admit I rarely seek out quotes in a time of victory. Quotes, for me, are about the journey. In short, they inspire me to get there, wherever there is. They pat my back, hug me, light a fire under my ass, tell me to get up or shut up. Most importantly, they tell me not to give up.

And for some reason, when my family was going through our seriously grave times a few years ago, Richard Nixon's words made semi-regular appearances on our quote board.

Oh, sure, we had the quotes you might expect, too.

"I get pretty impatient with people who are able-bodied

but are somehow paralyzed for other reasons."—Christopher Reeve

"Life shrinks or expands according to one's courage." -Anais Nin

"The greater the difficulty, the greater the glory." -Cicero

"Fate itself is like a wonderful, wide fabric in which every thread is guided by an infinitely tender hand and laid alongside another thread and is held and supported by a hundred others." -Rilke

"When you turn the corner and run into yourself, then you know that you have turned all the corners that are left." -Langston Hughes

"Confront boldness by being still more bold." -Napoleon.

And my husband's mantra during his twenties and early thirties—one of the reasons I went wild for him:

"Some folks hide, and some folks seek, and seeking, when it's mindless, neurotic, desperate, or pusillanimous can be a form of hiding. But there are folks who want to know and aren't afraid to look and won't turn tail should they find it—and if they never do, they'll have a good time anyway because nothing, neither the terrible truth not the absence of it, is going to cheat them out of one honest breath of earth's sweet gas."-Tom Robbins, *Still Life with Woodpecker*

All of these were tremendously helpful—putting wind into our sails on days when we felt nothing other than hot, dead air.

Of course, I realize that for many people on both sides of the political aisle, Richard Nixon is hardly someone whose wisdom you want to trot out in polite company.

To be honest, it started out as a joke—a little black humor that infused our moods like a change of music. My parents and grandparents were and are big fans of our 37th president, and like most people of our generation, we've been skeptical of their hero in ways we haven't been of other divisive figures they admire—Truman, Churchill, Reagan.

Years ago, when I was rolling my eyes and getting on my grandmother's case for her Nixon worship, she said to me, "Other than Watergate, what do you know about President Nixon?"

The truth was . . . nothing. Other than some such whatever about opening up China, blah, blah, blah.

A few days later, a package containing *Leaders* arrived on our doorstep in San Francisco. It was like receiving intellectual porn, and we hid the book on our shelf, careful to turn the spine so that no one could read what it said.

Later, my grandmother called.

"A real thinker samples from every variety of thought," she said.

I really do love it when people force me to think outside of my smug, little box. I not only turned *Leaders* around so that our visitors could see it when they walked into our living room, but actually took it off the shelf and read it.

Because regardless of how things turned out in Mr. Nixon's case—and admittedly, they turned out bad—the fact is, the man knew something about survival. And so did my grandmother.

And in his own, quirky way he provided levity and yes, even motivation during some of our very bleakest moments. His presence on our quote board was a great conversation starter when we had company and the inevitable question came—"Can I ask you why you're quoting Richard Nixon?"

In a house where Mr. Nixon's reminiscences about

Khrushchev, de Gaulle, and MacArthur sit comfortably on a shelf with the musings of Noam Chomsky, Hunter S. Thompson, David Brooks and Christopher Hitchens, the answer should be obvious.

But now that the good times are back—at least for a while—we can put Mr. Nixon away and take comfort in other words of wisdom.

"Nobody is bored when he is trying to make something that is beautiful, or to discover something that is true." -William Inge

Heavy sigh.

"If you can't annoy somebody, there's little point to writing." -Kingsley Amis

Uh-huh.

"Go confidently in the direction of your dreams. Live the life you've imagined." -Thoreau

"Follow your bliss." -Joseph Campbell

Yes.

But I will always hold a special place in my heart for a certain angry, brilliant, disgraced, strong, corrupt, and groundbreaking politician. Reading his books helped me understand my parents better, love them deeper. Nixon's role in the Cold War shaped their lives as his understanding of Russia and China was unmatched by any other American president. His domestic shenanigans were forgivable to people who had clawed their way over the Iron Curtain—even if to us, on the other side, Watergate was not only like learning Santa wasn't real, but that the adorable guy who played him at the mall was actually a drunk creep who kept his furry, red pants unzipped while you whispered your dreams into his ear.

Still, I have to hand it to Mr. Nixon. He not only gave me a mischievous laugh right when I really needed one, but challenged my perceptions and forced nuance into some of my most steadfast opinions.

As the left-leaning Senator Daniel Patrick Moynihan once observed, "The most liberal democratic administration in the second half of the 20th century was Richard Nixon's first term. Between 1968 and 1972, Mr. Nixon expanded welfare benefits, fortified civil rights for women and minorities, and created the EPA."

So, maybe I'm being a little too hasty in erasing Mr. Nixon's words from our quote board.

"Only if you have been in the deepest valley, can you ever know how magnificent it is to be on the highest mountain."

"Defeat does not finish a man, quit does. A man is not finished when he's defeated. He's finished when he quits."

"The finest steel has to go through the hottest fire."

He may still have plenty of wisdom to impart. The least of which filters through people I love who happen to love him. In my family's long and complicated history with President Nixon, the best thing to come out of it is a piece of sage advice. I won't go so far as to urge you to take it, but I'm going to do my damnedest to try in this coming year:

It's never too late to give someone a second chance.

Odd Little Post-Mother's Day Thoughts

On the morning of Mother's Day, my son brought home a tiny, premature snake. I mean this thing was only a little bit bigger than a matchstick and wiggled his glossy body all over my kid's fingers, biting them in a pathetic attempt at defending himself from what he imagined was a huge, goofy-grinned predator.

Charlie, I started calling him.

"It's so sad," my son said. "His mother was run over by a car and she was pregnant. Most of the baby snakes got smashed, too, but about four or five of them were squished out of her and survived."

We took Charlie to our kitchen and fed him a little egg yolk before my son set him free in some bushes by our porch. The critter would have to fend for himself, as our pet snake, Felina, is not the nurturing type. Some months ago she tried to smother her own brother, Pickles, and seems quite happy to have her habitat to herself now, thank you very much.

Charlie was sweet, and almost cute. We hated to let him go like that, but we needed to do it quickly before he got used to being taken care of and my son got attached. The itty-bitty thing, smaller than a worm, slithered away without a hint of sentiment for the boy who'd saved his life.

"Such is the plight of the mother," I told my son.
In response, he wrote me this Mother's Day poem:
Roses are red
Windex is blue
Thanks for cleaning my poo
I really appreciate it.

Smart-assed thirteen-year-old boy poems aside, I'm grateful to have had a much, much better Mother's Day than Charlie's mother. My husband and kids took me for a picnic by a trout lake nestled in a valley that looks up at the Blue Ridge Mountains. We ate Spanish ham French-style, with fresh baguettes, Manchego cheese, and a container of bright green olives that looked like miniature Granny Smith apples. We took a drive in our Jeep top down, and allowed ourselves to get sunburned. It was a nearly flawless day, our good fortune brought into even greater relief by Charlie and the fate of his mother and siblings.

And as we pulled into our driveway at the end of this wonderful excursion, the words of an author friend of mine popped into my head. I had to go searching for them in my quotes file, as I'd loved them so much I actually saved them there, waiting to re-purpose them. This whole Charlie episode presented a perfect opportunity.

"I came into the world kicking, screaming and covered in blood. I have no problem leaving the same way." -Khalid Muhammad, posted on Facebook some weeks ago.

Because ain't that the truth? This birthing business, whether you're on the giving end or the receiving end, isn't for the faint-hearted. It's beautiful and terrible and thrilling. It's dangerous.

Nothing has given me more satisfaction than being a mother and nothing has made me feel more insignificant. From the moment I looked into my first child's eyes—the above mentioned son—I knew my life was over. Even if only metaphorically speaking. I became fully aware that if I did this thing right, I would put his interests above my own and go on to raise an independent, competent human being, who would learn the skills to leave me behind and build his own happy life with a family of his choice and making. Hopefully, he would look over his shoulder every once in a while—unlike Charlie, that ungrateful bastard—and shoot me a wistful smile. A "thanks for cleaning my poo" smile.

And hopefully, he and his sisters will take notice of how much I appreciate my own mom, who not only gave me life, but a good one at that. All I have to do is watch the news for five minutes to know how lucky I am to have her. Or just look at Charlie, who has to go it alone in this world.

[love the grit]

Snowy Days Amidst Love And Death

We had a snow storm last week, which I wouldn't go so far as to say is rare in Virginia, but happens infrequently enough to plunge our whole county into a dithering mess. No one knows how to drive in the snow, there aren't enough plows to go around, and it feels like pretty much everyone just throws their hands in the air, lights a fire, and gives up.

Case in point, school was canceled for the entire week, and my kids only made it back yesterday on a two-hour delay, even though a fifty-five degree day over the weekend had rendered whatever roads were still icy and snowy just slushy and wet, but drive-able.

All of this would have been fine—fun, even—if I hadn't started writing a YA romance that has just been consuming me in my waking hours.

When I say romance, I'm not talking teen Harlequin. I mean epic romance in the tradition of *Dr. Zhivago* and *Jane Eyre*. I'm scraping the depths of my soul for this, turning my heart inside out and back again, summoning every poetic romanticism that has ever made me shiver, cry, lose my breath.

I've been thinking a lot about love—how it enters our lives, what to do with it when it does, how to hold it dear. The chipped, empty bowl we can find ourselves holding at the end of our days if we squander it.

My new fixation, however, is not the departure from Cold War shenanigans and brutal dictators that it looks like. In fact, like most of my stories, it has its roots in the everyday goings on in my family.

You see, I've been watching my mom care for my dad as he's dying. Sometimes seeing this hands-on, and other times from another time zone away, but nevertheless, at the very least we talk every day and I get a detailed rundown of what's going on.

My dad is ninety-four, twenty-two years her senior, and has been a force of nature all of his life. He's cranky, brilliant, has a spine stiff enough to brave world wars, and a heart big enough to put us first. And he has fought tooth and nail his reversal of fortune from doctor to patient.

"Don't help me!" he said, as my mom and I were trying to lift him into bed after he'd collapsed a couple of weeks ago in his and my mom's Chicago townhouse.

"Dad," I said. "This is love. It's why I'm here."

He was naked and embarrassed and in pain.

"Thank you," he said, barely above a whisper.

His decline has been swift since then, and he has become interned in the very hospital where he was once chief of staff. He feels loved there, and they treat him like a legend. But that doesn't mean he likes it.

My mom has been cooking his meals and bringing them to his hospital room, so that he can feel like he's at home—sort of. He's always liked her cooking. And although he is capable of being her harshest critic, he has been gazing upon her with the love and adoration of a teenage crush.

This is certainly my most intimate experience with watching someone close to me die. It is as harrowing as it is breath-taking—like a dazzling sunset observed in the cold, your fingers freezing and your ears numb. No coat.

And it is precisely my experiences with death and near death in the past few years that have gotten me thinking about love enough to inspire me to write about it in a big way. My daughter's catastrophic illness, my grandmother's death, and now my dad's.

All of it feels like it's happened in such a short time.

My sister-in-law has recently been through the end of life dance with her in-laws as well, and my husband and I have been privy to a play-by-play that has helped us prepare for what is going on with my dad.

That has been a blessing, as has the love story that unfolded before us.

Alice was one hundred and one years old and Al was ninety-seven. Both sharp as a tack, Alice was still doing the *New York Times* crossword puzzle every day the week she died. "See you Tuesday," Alice's nurse said at the end of what would be her final visit. Alice looked up from her puzzle and said, "I don't think so."

She died in her sleep the next night.

Their caregivers didn't want to wake Al until they absolutely had to. Al and Alice had been together for over seventy-five years and they figured he would need as much rest as possible before having to face that she was gone.

When they did wake him, he held her hand and called her his sweetheart. He spoke to his wife as if they were courting, telling her in sweet detail how much he loved her. Their caregivers sobbed with Al and held him close as Alice's body was taken away.

In the following weeks, Al started to forget things. Mostly, he would forget that Alice had died. He would become frantic looking for her, and my sister-in-law and her husband would have to sit him down and explain that she was gone. The hardest part was that he would relive her death each time they told him, as if he was hearing the news for the first time.

This is love.

And this is why, as I endeavored to write the agonizing and beautiful truth about love in my story, and as my kids interrupted me every five minutes - driving me crazy, not letting me get any good work done, not letting me sift through my own grief and conflicting emotions about my dad's death and my mom's ordeal in caring for him, about the changes in all of our lives as she prepares to move down to Virginia and into our house after he passes - I wanted to scream! Between their stomach flus and my dad being sick way over in Chicago and my traveling there, and now the snow days, I was so behind on everything and I was not in the best of emotional shape. To top it all off, just as I'd shooed the little buggers away and finally settled down into my story, my husband comes in and says, "I'm just starving. Can you make me that thing with the cheese and the oil and vinegar vegetables—I've got such a taste for that." Like he doesn't have a pair of hands.

"That thing. You mean a sandwich?" I said.

Just before I was about to hurl some other smart-ass comment, I started to laugh at myself. Here I was writing about love. Getting horribly exasperated about being thwarted from giving such an important topic the thought that I needed in order to make it come alive on the page— and I was on the brink of telling everyone I love to leave me the hell alone for once in their miserable lives. I put my face into my hands.

"What?" my husband said.

I shook my head.

Then I got up and made his sandwich.

Because this is love.

Heartland

My dad died last week.
Contemplating what exactly life will look like after the passing of a close family member is a bit like staring at one of those thousand-piece jigsaw puzzles. You know you've got to start somewhere, but all you want to do is close up the box, put it back on the shelf and go do something mindless, like watch bad TV.

But you can't.

So, after the hugs and the hearty bowls of chicken paprika, my family and I started with just one puzzle piece—my dad's briefcase.

This wasn't one of those fancy attaché numbers. It was a simple leather case that had been bought probably around 1971 and contained the precious knick-knacks of a long, complex life. One filled with gold and bronze medals of accomplishment, dozens of pairs of *Mad Men*-era cuff links—gold initials in wide font, giant topaz ovals, classic onyx rectangles—all left-over from a time when professional men wore French cuffs almost every single day of their lives. And oh, the tie pins: a golf club, an American flag, a jumbo jet from when flying was glamorous. Twenty or so stamps hand-picked for a collection that never quite got off the ground. Certificates of authenticity, letters of thanks, and tiny tokens from a medical practice that spanned more than six decades—a pocket watch, a plaque, a silver pen with an inscription that read simply, "Doc."

A collection of treasures unmistakably from a certain time, but also from a certain place. In both tone and style, my dad's personal effects were decidedly Midwestern. In other words, lacking irony, restraint, snobbery and chic. Brimming over with the pride of having made it, and the humility of knowing that it could all be taken away any moment.

My dad came to Chicago from Europe on the heels of the Second World War. Like many immigrants, he came without a penny to his name and actually slept on a park bench and ate at soup kitchens for weeks before he got his first paycheck.

"Can you imagine?" he once told me. "By day I was performing surgeries at a big hospital. People saying 'yes, doctor, no, doctor,' and at night, I lived like a bum. But I liked the fresh air and you know, you do what you have to do."

I really did think I was prepared for my dad's passing. Not just for the void it would leave in my life, the closing of a chapter, but also the changes his death would visit upon my family. My mom will be moving in with us as soon as she's able to tie up loose ends. She'll be leaving the town outside of Chicago where I grew up, where she landed as a Czech immigrant in 1968. And she'll be making her home in a semi-rural crossroads just outside of a college town in Virginia. That's quite a change. And I want to help her through it without big-footing her and pushing her to do things she's not ready for. Like taking a yoga class or making a friend.

I do know something about grief. That we think we're fine and end up acting out of character—forgetting entire conversations, spacing out people we've met a half dozen times, missing appointments. Grief makes you revisit the past and thrusts you into the future all at the same time. It's bewildering, scary and oddly exhilarating. Missing pieces of your own puzzle turn up in places you never expected—a song you never particularly liked, a friend you've long since let slip away, a picture from a family vacation you can't even recall.

With the loss of my dad, I have quite suddenly been hit with the fact that I will be losing my strongest tether to the Midwest, a region which I've come to realize has shaped me as much as my family culture, my ethnicity, my gender, my friends, and even my spouse and children.

It's why I'll talk up anyone in any old grocery line, tell them I like their hair and ask them about what they did over the weekend. Why —no matter how busy I am—I still feel a little weird about having someone else clean my house. Even if they only do it every couple of weeks. Even if I love it. My Midwestern upbringing is why I just can't bring myself to get all that excited about the Ivy League. I'm not knocking it, I've just known too many immigrants, self-starters and non-academic intellectuals to place too much stock in rarefied institutions. And it's why my European friends have always told me that I don't seem American. I've tried to explain to them that it is less because I'm a European's kid than I am a heartland girl. Europeans mostly know American media and television shows, and those come from the coasts. People from the heartland are an entirely different animal.

In the scant few days my husband, children and I spent helping my mother make the initial transition from wife to widow, the patently uncool charm of my birthplace felt pure and comforting. It was a warm towel fresh out of the dryer.

I loved being waited on at the Nordstrom cosmetics counter by a young, balding woman with a skin disease, and that it didn't seem in the least bit odd. And being greeted at the hostess desk at a swanky restaurant by two retired women instead of the usual hip, nubile young things that smile and ask you to follow their shapely derrieres to your table. I loved demonstrating to my baffled children that I know how to bowl. My high school still has a bowling team, for goodness' sake. I loved that guys—young or old—would never miss the opportunity to hold the door open for me, give me their seat.

And I love that my dad was crazy about gangster movies, but when I gave him a boxed set of *The Sopranos* a few years ago, he threw every one of the DVDs in the trash.

"It's where they belong," he said.

My dad was a cultured man who spoke five languages, had an M.D. and a PhD, knew classical literature and classical music and certainly knew good content, but he just couldn't appreciate what he called "filth masquerading as art."

That is a solidly Midwestern trait.

But don't let it fool you.

Heartlanders love dirty jokes and knocking back a few drinks. The Playboy empire was started in Chicago, after all, before migrating to the West Coast. My dad himself married a vivacious woman more than twenty years his junior, even if she did tell his friends that she was a good five years older than she actually was.

And for all of its chivalry and down-to-earth warmth, many Midwesterners are horrible, aggressive drivers. Especially Chicagoans. They speed, zip in and out of lanes, fly through yellow lights at the last minute, cut you off with a fist in the air and a string of curses they'd rarely employ anywhere but inside their automobiles.

Even after twenty years of living with and loving me, my husband still can't stand my driving.

And as we pulled away from my mom's townhouse at the end of the week—merely slowing down at the stop sign at the end of her street, then pulling out right in front of another minivan, forcing that driver to hit his breaks—there was that wistful feeling of satisfaction, a woebegone sense of fulfillment that a portion of that enormous puzzle of grief had been laid. The heartland piece.

Only about eight-hundred and fifty more to go.

My Kind Of Town
The Glories Of Chicago In The Cold

My husband has been having a lot of business trips to Chicago lately, which has got me thinking about my home town. The gray, snow-heavy skies, the smokestacks, the way Lake Michigan freezes over this time of year—a veritable tundra flanked by a glittering skyline that looks like it's made of Legos.

I love Chicago in the winter.

And no, I'm not some sort of masochist who enjoys being whipped by gale-force icy winds, have my tears frozen to my cheeks and my toes . . . wait, what toes? I can't feel them anymore.

So, I should clarify. Being a visitor there at this time of year just sucks. All you want to do is curl up in your hotel room and thank God that you live somewhere else. What I'm lonesome for is living in Chicago during the winter. And those are two very different things.

I will preface this by pointing out that summer is magnificent there. The city comes alive with the purpose and voracity of an ant hill. There are blues fests and jazz fests and food fests and lakeside beach parties and all manner of good times had. It's a walking city with great architecture, and people sit out on their stoops, talking to neighbors or just any old passersby. I was sitting on a friend's stoop some years ago when a guy ran out of an Irish bar across the street and hollered, "The Bulls just won the championship!" Stores, restaurants and homes emptied in a rush as a spontaneous parade ensued—joyful, uncontainable—continuing all the way downtown. So, the summer does indeed have magic.

But the winter is special. It has its own vibe and exists only for those in the know.

I love the grit, the ugliness of the winter. The way the snow turns black and the stockyards empty, looking like they'd come victim to a dirty bomb. The way there are so many Buicks still on the road.

And the fact that everyone shrugs off the cold. As a kid, I had only a handful of snow days and they were always just after some mammoth blizzard. But as soon as the tire chains were on, our parents would wrap us up from head to toe and send us out into the arctic chill. At recess, we would actually play a game where my friends and I would spit high into the air, just to watch our lugies shatter when they hit the ground. It was so damned cold our saliva froze in midair.

Winter is when Chicagoans are at their best.

Like when my roommate brought home some Australian tourist who'd been locked out of his hostel after missing the midnight curfew. And no, it wasn't a hook-up. It was a kindness. "I hope you don't mind," she said. I didn't. We set him up on our couch, gave him a key, and let him come and go for the next few days—just to save him some money. My roommate even lent him her car.

It's just how we roll there.

He hung out with our friends, we let him tag along to all of the best places nobody knows about, cooked some of his meals, and made giant bowls of popcorn as we entertained ourselves to the sounds of our neighbors' screaming fights—a favorite past-time in my first post-college household.

"I'm gonna have you killed!"

"You don't have the wit to have me killed, you moron."

"Shut up!"

"You shut up!"

"What do ya want for dinner?"

"Let's get Chinese."

(This was an actual exchange. I wrote it down in my journal)

All of this was during a deep freeze, too. They happen at least once a year, when the temperatures plunge to about twenty-six degrees below zero without wind-chill. The poor, Aussie bloke had chosen to come to Chicago at the worst possible time. He was traveling in America for most of the year and for reasons that defy logic, made his way up from Florida instead of continuing laterally and staying snuggly in the South. Yet at the end of it all, when he sent us a Christmas card the following year, he wrote that the time he spent in the Windy City was by far the best he had during his whole trip.

And I believe him.

He was welcomed into a subculture that not a lot of outsiders get to see. A tribe of urban dwellers who, no matter how God-awful the weather, endeavor to go out and have a ball. The bars and restaurants jam, the invitations go out, the parties rage. People tear up the night with gusto.

It's why Chicago winters are responsible for some of my fondest memories.

Like hitting the blues bars on the South Side as a teen and taking for granted the legends on the stage. Because truth be told, we were there to indulge in some under-age drinking, and those bars would accept your grandmother's expired driver's license. Heck, they'd take a note from your grandmother that read, *Please let Billy drink alcohol tonight. He's over twenty-one—swear.*

Chicago is marvelously, unapologetically corrupt.

It's also romantic. Underneath the scarves and the sweaters and the down jackets lay burning hearts.

I remember drinking whiskey with my future husband at a one-time speakeasy, listening to a live three-piece jazz ensemble into the wee hours and reading scratch graffiti from Al Capone's day. We fell in love in Chicago, mostly during the winter, and spent countless chilly nights at everywhere from dive bars to champagne bars, seducing each other with off-color humor that would make people on the coasts shudder. And made the people around us snicker and buy us drinks.

Because Chicago is like that. It's down to earth, no bullshit. And her citizens have retained their sense of humor. They eat big, they laugh big, they drink big. And if they like you, you'll get a helluva lot more out of them then the polite albeit interesting conversations you'll encounter on the cocktail circuits of New York and San Francisco. Not that I'm knocking those. They have their own excitement and make you feel like you're part of the glitterati.

It's just that a Chicagoan will make you feel like you're a part of a family. He'll have you take your shoes off in his house for comfort, tell you a story, offer you a bedroom in case you over-indulge, and hug you when you leave. Hug you tight.

In spirit, what's called "the lake effect" extends far beyond the drastic swings in weather chronicled by the city's meteorologists. An infinite expanse of sky, along with a history of dirty-underhanded dealings, fires, massacres, and machine politics has created a population that can take it—whatever it is.

In that light, a little sub-zero weather is nothing.

In fact, it's an opportunity for spontaneous acts of generosity—like scraping the ice off a neighbor's windshield in the dawn hours, leaving a heavy dumpling meal for a friend with a nasty cold, helping a frightened, dithering lady push her car out of a snowy ditch while you're wearing your good shoes.

It's those things that keep moods light during the grim winter months, bring people together, give them something to root for. The cold is as binding to that city's soul as alcohol and music. It is there to break down walls in a place that could otherwise be just a hard, industrial wilderness. The cruel nights and bleak, unforgiving days smooth the way for what really makes Chicago hum and hiss and pitter and pat when most towns stop dead in their tracks, leaving citizens to hole up in their homes until the snow melts. They nurture real human interaction, great talks. The kinds of heart-to-hearts that don't let you get away with not giving yourself away. That turn an acquaintance into a true friend.

I guess that's what I miss most about Chicago winters. It's their warmth.

[having it all]

Sundays With Merle

Years ago, my Aunt Viki and Uncle George owned a small, cheerful retirement home near Tampa, Florida. It was called Park Manor and was made up of mostly middle-class old folks who more often than not felt some connection to my family's Czech heritage.

Viki and George, although only in their early forties at the time, were like mom and dad at this place—and they got to know each and every one of the people who chose to make their lovely, little assisted living facility their home.

As you can imagine, there were a lot of unforgettable characters at Park Manor: The octogenarian former beauty queen who slinked around in low-cut party dresses by day and transparent negligees by night. She had a huge crush on my then-twenty-two-year-old brother and used to invite him to her, ahem, room. Then, there were the warring Czech brides. Fifty years earlier, one had run off with the other one's husband, and they hadn't seen each other since. In the kind of twist of fate that proves God really does have a sense of humor, these ladies were made roommates at Park Manor. Ignorant of their past, my aunt figured that since they both spoke Czech, they'd make fast friends. Instead, they had to be placed in opposite wings, or else be found rolling on the floor, pulling each other's hair out.

But of all the lovebirds, the wicked witches, the playboys,

the card sharks, the war heroes, the comedians, and the master bakers, none was more memorable than Merle.

At one hundred years old, Merle stood slender and erect, with only the help of a hand-carved cane. Short gray hair, equally gray eyes that twinkled like deep water on an overcast day. Neat, comfortable clothes, no make-up other than lipstick—"You can't forget you're a woman," she'd say.

Merle had been married twice and widowed twice. Always ready for a laugh at her own expense, she displayed on her night table a come-hither picture of herself—taken by her second husband, on her second wedding night. In it, she was seventy-five years of age, and looked pretty darned good in a long, black, silky nightgown with her hair swept up.

She always had a story, and I never heard a single negative word come out of her mouth on any of my visits. And this was a woman who'd lived through World War I, The Great Depression, World War II, Segregation, The Cold War, Vietnam—Jimmy Carter, for goodness sake, she used to say (although always in good humor).

But the most extraordinary thing about Merle was expressed on Sunday afternoons.

Sundays at Park Manor were by far the most popular visiting days, as many families chose to stop in for lunch after church. By mid-afternoon or so, many visitors would start to take their leave. There were dinners to be made, and old folks get tired.

But at Merle's, the party was just getting started.

Nearly every single Sunday, Merle's room was so filled with visitors that many had to linger in the hall and take turns going in. Boisterous laughter, children's squeals and just about any style of music—ragtime, swing, rock-n-roll—echoed throughout Merle's wing. Her children, grandchildren and great-grandchildren from her first marriage were there, but so were her second husband's children. Although she couldn't have met them until they were well into middle age themselves, she'd made inroads into their hearts and counted her second husband's grandchildren as hers, too.

And everyone stayed up to the minute visiting hours ended.

I guess I paid such close attention to Merle because of the wasted love I'd seen in my own family. I'd watched too many loved ones give away the ties that bind like they were twenty-five-cent raffle tickets. They ran from their mistakes in their young lives, and kept running throughout midlife and even beyond. It seemed to work for them. By and large, they were free to live lives unencumbered by the inconveniences that true emotional responsibility can visit upon a life.

And they remained free of the benefits as well, always appearing vaguely uncomfortable when faced with the gush of a happy child's love, or a chance view of a tender kiss stolen between a husband and wife at a crowded family gathering.

And sooner or later, they simply ended up. Not always alone, per se. There are brothers and sisters and friends that sometimes step in. The void, I suppose, is present mostly in the memories they never collected.

I remember my aunt telling me that her experience at Park Manor had taught her that the majority of people who ended up alone on Sunday after Sunday had earned it. I found that to be a devastating revelation.

Shortly after Merle finally died, my aunt and uncle got an offer they couldn't refuse. It was from a large convalescent home chain, and sewed up their own hard-earned retirement. It was tough for them to let go because my aunt and uncle really cared about the people at Park Manor and had looked out for their dignity, their quality of life. On their last day, the place was filled with house-made chocolate pudding and tears.

Later, my aunt admitted to me that she could have never sold the place while Merle was still alive.

That Merle. Considering I only met her a handful of times, she's had a pretty disproportionate effect on the way I view my life. When I find myself wallowing over my usual litany of complaints—undoubtedly revolving around childcare, work, and a lack of *me* time—Merle often pops into my mind.

I'm sure I romanticize her to some extent, and that there are people out there who might tell a whole different story about the way she conducted her life—one that reveals her human foibles. Like if she got piss-drunk before the school play, then heckled the entire seventh grade cast of *The Importance of Being Earnest*, or called her Aunt June a whore during Thanksgiving dinner, or threatened to leave her husband for their son's history teacher, perhaps.

But even if all those things were true, I'd still hold her up as a gold standard. The way I want to end up.

Merle's example has served as a lifelong reminder to me that the benefits of love accrue. Even when we mess up spectacularly, it's worth going back for more, trying to right what we've done wrong. Merle's life seemed to exemplify that. How could she not have given so much more than she got, seeing the devotion she inspired, long after her family had stopped needing her, after all?

Merle seemed to embrace the sad and wonderful truth about the human family. That the people under your roof are not happier when you're more fulfilled, when your time is respected. They're happier when you go out of your way for them. When you drop what you're doing to have a laugh and a kiss.

The same way I'll be happier if my children set aside their Sundays for me when I'm in my own version of Park Manor—one that hopefully includes a travel club, barre classes and rabid boxing fans. Maybe a couple of dance halls and a tiki bar. A cowboy or two.

Because even if my son and daughters are crazy busy and have cupcakes to make for a bake sale, or a big presentation at work due early that Monday morning, I want them in my room—laughing, talking, listening to music. Fighting to take their turn from the hallway.

What's In A Name?

My name is Victoria and it has never felt right to me.

Not when I was a kid and my friends called me Vic or Vicki, nor when my family called me Vikinka or Viktorka or any derivative of my more formal moniker.

Right around when I hit college, people stopped calling me by nicknames entirely and Victoria was settled on for good. While it was definitely more consistent, it still felt neither here nor there.

It's funny, even after the long-form "Victoria" became pretty much the only version of my name people used, there was a whole cadre of people who just always got my name wrong. For reasons I can't explain, a lot of folks have simply called me Veronica—even after I've corrected them numerous times.

They say, "Right, right, it's Victoria—of course. I'm sorry, Veronica."

Weird.

Or maybe not so much.

About a year ago, my mother made an illuminating admission to me. She told me how much she hadn't wanted to name me Victoria at all. How after I was born, she could hardly even say my name. And when she did, no matter how hard she tried, no matter how many ways—Vic-toria, Vic-tor-i-a, Vic-tor-ia—the name always tripped over her tongue tinged with a note of bitterness.

I'd had a brother named Victor, you see. He'd died of the flu the year before I was born. So, back when I was a baby, and my mom's suffering was still so fresh, my name was simply too painful for her to say.

It may seem strange that my mom gave me the name Victoria in the first place—that perhaps it was some form of masochism on her part. Because really, couldn't she have given me another name?

My mother said she'd wanted to give me an Italian name, actually. After fleeing communist Czechoslovakia, she'd spent several months in an Italian refugee camp. Her belly felt my first kick in the countryside near Positano, and my other brother, John—eight years old at the time, had his baptism in Rome. She made many friends there while she waited for permission to come to America. Italy was the first place that made my mom smile after Victor's death.

And Italy was her stepping stone to America.

My mother had spent most of her life dreaming about a life in America. But not merely for the usual reasons—freedom of speech and expression, freedom to travel, social mobility, freedom from random imprisonment and other forms of persecution, etc. My mother's reasons were more personal.

America was where my mother's parents, Bedriska and Victor, lived. They'd fled Czechoslovakia when my mom was only six and my mother had spent twenty years pining for them. She'd risked her life and her surviving children's—mine (in utero) and John's—to escape from behind the Iron Curtain.

My mother wanted desperately to have a relationship with her parents. They had loomed so large, for so long in her imagination. She had envisaged what it would be like baking koláčky with her mother, shopping for a dress, just being held by her.

She wondered what her father's muscular hands might look like opening a difficult jar of pickles, or feel like if he were to stroke her hair. Both of my grandparents were physically imposing—my grandfather, an Olympic hockey player, was built like a Sherman tank. Victor was a name that suited him very well. My grandmother, tall and beautiful, could have been Greta Garbo's sister. Bedriska—Fredericka in English—was a name she owned.

In those first few, heady months they were back together, my mother was starstruck by her parents. Everything they said held tremendous weight. My mother had come from a communist country and out of fear had hidden her opinions all of her life. And here, in this new, free country, her parents had opinions about everything and shared them willy-nilly. They talked about which politicians they preferred, their plans for the future, things they liked and didn't like about their adopted country . . .

And the names they wanted my mother to bestow upon her unborn child.

My grandparents were determined that my mom should name me after her sisters, Victoria (named after my grandfather) and Helen. At the time, Victoria and Helen were still stuck behind the Iron Curtain, and my grandparents—perhaps—felt an homage to them was in order. My grandmother and grandfather had never met my deceased brother and I don't think it occurred to them that the similarities between Victor and Victoria would cause my mom such grief.

And at the time, my mother didn't have it in her to speak up for herself. So, reluctantly, with a forced smile, she agreed to name me Victoria Helen.

My mom's story of how I came to be "Victoria" explains a lot, especially in terms of my own ambivalence towards my name. Honestly, even now when people ask me how I prefer to be addressed—whether by Victoria or Vic or Vicki—my inner voice always answers, "I don't really care—pick one." Then I say out loud, "Victoria is fine."

And while name issues have played a pretty insignificant role in my life, I do find it interesting how my mother's unspoken feelings about my name seem to have affected my own perceptions about what I am called. Victoria has always felt like a name that was thrust upon me instead of given me.

And I think about how differently I feel about the names of people who are dear to me. My husband, Jack, my children.

I remember seeing my babies' names for the first time, written down on an official document at the hospital shortly after I gave birth. It was a powerful experience to behold their names in black and white. It made them real. I remember my husband running his fingers over our son's name and saying it aloud with tears in his eyes.

Our daughters' names felt no less significant. We'd spent months going back and forth about what to call them. With each of our children, we waited until they were born and we'd looked into their murky eyes before deciding which name to give them. Naturally, we'd narrowed it down to two possibilities for each sex, but we wanted to see our babies first—just to make sure we were making the right choice.

And each time it was so clear.
Eamon.
Charlotte.
Josephine.

They could have had no other names.

It just makes me ache that my mother was denied that experience. That my name is a forever reminder of her greatest heartbreak—my brother's death, instead of her greatest triumph—her courageous escape from Czechoslovakia.

And I hope that being able to choose her own American name—even if it was a direct translation of her Czech name—was in some way a consolation. Georgiana is her American name. And she does love it. Jirina, her Czech name, only exists for her now in the old country, on her old documents, on a list of Czech political prisoners from the 1950s and 60s. It endures in the abstract for my mother, like an old address.

As for my name, I still don't really care much. It means something, I suppose, when I see Victoria Dougherty written on the cover of my novel, but I might use a different name when I publish in the Young Adult category next year.

If I do, perhaps I should ask my mother to give me a nom de plume. Something Italian.

The Never-Ending Surprise Party

I was cooking dinner when my husband called. He'd already been gone for ten days on this punishing, potato sack race of an international business trip and still had another week to go. So, I just couldn't contain myself when his number came up on my phone. I mean, really, I jumped up and down.

I always look forward to hearing his quirky stories and cranky observations, especially when he's far, far away. Since having children, I've become mostly an armchair traveler, so his musings about foreign countries I know—Ireland, England, Germany—and don't know—Russia—were not only going to be a fun distraction for me, but a chance for us to connect and have a laugh, help me miss him less.

"What are you cookin'?" he asked.

"Chicken with lemon rice." It's a family favorite.

"Yes!" he said. "You slow-roasted the chicken, right? I mean, you didn't cheat?"

Of course I cheated. I'm single-parenting until next Saturday and don't have time to baste a chicken for three hours. "Cheat? Me?"

"Because my day took an unexpected turn this morning," he continued. "And I'm going to be home in an hour."

I got all verklempt.

"Are you crying?" he asked me.

Honestly, since having children I cry watching cat food

commercials, but I really was so happy that he was on his way home. And I love that he kept it from me until the last minute. That our son's jaw was going to drop, then morph into a grin like a fat orange slice when he saw his dad come waltzing in. That our daughters would squeal. Well, one of them anyway. The other one gets all pre-teen and says mushy things like, "Hey, Dad."

As a family, we have always celebrated surprises. We take spur of the moment trips to podunk towns that do or do not turn out to be fun, we reach out to new neighbors, we move, we buy old houses, dream up schemes and stories, have more kids than we planned, don't want to know the sex of our babies until they're born, take on too many projects and surrender to rotten, good-for-nothing luck, not just in the hopes of surviving it, but with the belief that in the end something special will come out of our long, dark journey. Like a new best friend or a golden, once-in-a-lifetime opportunity. Or maybe just some wisdom and empathy.

All, not most, of the best things in my life have come from surprises, so I'm not just being a Pollyanna here. The Berlin Wall coming down was a huge surprise, as was my decision to move to Prague shortly after. Falling in love with my husband came so far out of left field that I still find myself humming that Talking Heads song, where David Byrne sings about finding yourself in a beautiful house, with a beautiful wife and asking himself how he got there.

Every facet of having children has been surprising—from finding myself obsessed with their interests and emotions to a pitying degree, to how much and how little they are like me. People tell you a lot of things about becoming a parent, but nobody tells you that children will be a mirror held up to your soul—exposing the best and the worst of you, making you desperate to fix your own flaws for their sake. Selfishness, vanity, any sense of moral equivalency or ambiguity—at least in regard to their welfare—don't get thrown out the window, necessarily, but are definitely thrown a curve ball.

And no, sister, you can't have it all. You get so much more than having it all.

Plunging into the role of wife and mother has been a one-way ticket to being a better person for me. More than the accomplishments I craved like street drugs when I was growing up, more than therapy, more than seeking enlightenment. Not to beat a dead horse here, but that's been kind of surprising. It's been a one-way ticket in coach, mind you, on a train that often smells of perspiration, spilled cognac, cigarettes and live roosters, but damn, it takes you to the most unexpected, often glorious places.

And lately, I've been surprised at the daughter I'm becoming.

Although we always loved each other tremendously, my mom and I weren't actually close until my late thirties, when my youngest was born so sick. Without missing a beat, my mom kicked into overdrive. Her heroic efforts to ease our burden—taking the night shift at the hospital so that we could be with our other kids, massaging my feet after a shattering day, standing in for me at field trips and class parties—helped us both see each other anew. Since then I have slowly, sometimes painfully, in a cut-and-bleed, stitches-and-Band-Aids kind of way, become a daughter.

It has been a narrow and bumpy road.

I've had to surrender some of my prized independence, care for my mother without taking on a condescending or bossy air, and accept the fact as lovingly and graciously as

I can, that my littlest loves my mom more than anyone in the world.

More than she loves me.

Against everything that my younger self would have thought possible, I'm endeavoring to guide my mom through the twilight of her life—from the death of her husband to the change from her role as mistress of her own household, to being a part of mine. And I'm learning that I welcome and relish the challenge—most of the time. Even when I lose my temper and get it all wrong—which is often.

No surprise there.

I'm sharing my kitchen—which is huge for me—letting my mom rearrange things, throw out perfectly good mops in favor of her own, over-stuff my pantry, and serve us her "Chinese" food with a French baguette instead of rice.

"Mmm," I say, hoping she won't trot out her other "ethnic" dishes. Like spaghetti and meatballs served with a sauce of Campbell's tomato soup cut with milk. My mom spent seven months in an Italian refugee camp after fleeing Communist Czechoslovakia, and is the only person I know who loved everything about Italy except for the food.

But while her forays into international cuisine are dubious, she's actually a wonderful cook—when she's cooking Czech food. Her goulash, potato dumplings, schnitzel, and sweet and sour cabbage are a welcome shake-up of our family dinners. I can't wait to cook Thanksgiving and Christmas meals with her for the first time in years. Goose, mushrooms, fruit tarts, spaetzle.

And the best surprise of all is that I'm once again finding myself falling deeper in love with the man I married. A guy who is not only welcoming his mother-in-law into his home, but is creating two lovely smoking lounges for her on our front and back porches. A man who isn't afraid to be the bad guy when he needs to be—setting boundaries and confronting very real issues. Like when my mom contradicts our parenting, either behind our backs or right in front of the kids. From "Oh, come on, she can have another ice cream," (Not after chocolate chip cookies and a full bag of gummi worms she can't!) to "If Mama won't buy you a phone, I will," (What the @#$%&*!??)

"It'll take some adjustment," my husband says. "But we'll get to go away alone now, too—have overnight dates."

I'll get to tag along on business trips and expand my own career universe without feeling guilty for leaving for a couple of days.

"Most of all, it's a chance to grow," my husband reminds me.

A surprise always offers that chance—to those who are willing to embrace it.

Flat-Out Love

"Love is hard," people say. "Marriage isn't about romance."

I was at a panel about love on Saturday at the Virginia Festival of the Book and it got me thinking.

While love is most certainly one of my favorite topics, that's not why I went. Daniel Jones, the editor of the *New York Times* Modern Love column, has a new book out (*Love Illuminated*), and since I'd written a Modern Love essay a few years ago and found Daniel to be delightful and so very helpful to a novice essay writer like me, I wanted to go to the panel and buy his book. It was my small way of saying thanks.

Besides Daniel, two other authors shared the podium: a family lawyer and blogger who'd written a book about what it's really like to be a divorce lawyer, and a psychologist who is both a grief and a marriage counselor. The latter had written a book of tips on cultivating a happy marriage.

All of them were wonderful and had a lot of poignant things to say.

I learned from Daniel that many of the students who write to him feel lost and lonely in the current "hook-up" culture prevalent on today's college campuses. There is, after all, a poverty of soul to waking up next to someone you hardly know and getting a "well, I guess I'll see you around," after a night of passion instead of a loving smile, a kiss, and an "I'll see you after class."

He told stories about modern-day struggles to find a lasting relationship: the analysts who make tallies of pros and cons in their love prospects, and the romantics who bathe themselves in that magical potion of common sense and lust as they keep an eye out for "the one."

The psychologist spoke of the dichotomy between her grief and marriage counseling practices, and how much one informs the other. A full half of her patients are widows and widowers who are utterly heartbroken at their loss and would do anything to have their beloved back. Even if just for a scant minute—to tell them how much they love them.

The other half of her practice is made up of people who have in many cases squandered the most precious relationship in their lives through anything from adultery and abuse to negligence or mere nit-picking. They are now desperate and repentant, and confused and adrift, or hopeful and re-energized. Ready to make it work.

And last, the family lawyer took the podium. Her words were counterintuitive and romantic—yes, romantic. It was a privilege for her, she told us, to see people at their most raw and be privy in an intimate way to the fallout from their greatest personal failure. She has sat with men as they wept openly because they missed their children so badly. With women who shook with fear at the prospect of having to sell their house.

Yet at the end of the day, she said she still considers herself a love junkie despite the nature of her job. One who posts wedding pictures of former clients and their new families all over her office. Who holds a deep appreciation for her own happy marriage.

With love, the stakes are so huge—especially after love becomes marriage. There is no other relationship, as the psychologist pointed out, that combines all elements of the human experience: ardor, friendship, partnership, sexuality, blood, and death.

Could anything possibly be more important?

At the end of the hour, despite so many painful and gushing revelations, all the panelists agreed that love was not like a Disney movie or a romance novel. Not real love, anyway.

But I disagree.

For my part, I've sat and listened as a family friend talked about his wife of almost twenty years with a breathlessness that bordered on rapture. "She's all that matters," he said. "Her and our kids." And this was coming from a Marine Corps General who looks like a cross between Ed Harris and Bryan Cranston.

I've watched men and women shower their step-children with the same affection and financial resources that they had reserved for their own flesh and blood, and cry as those kids go off to a college they've mortgaged their house to pay for.

If that's not a Disney movie, I don't know what is.

In my own marriage, my husband and I say things to each other that would make most cultured people want to gag—Harlequin novel stuff, but hopefully with better dialogue.

It's that very fact that prompted our son—a typical glib, dirty-joke telling, tits-obsessed twelve-year-old to say to his buddy—in all seriousness—"Why won't you tell me who you like? It's nothing to be ashamed of." He paused and looked out the window. "Love is beautiful."

I'm glad his father and I have had something to do with

his perception of love and I'm not going to disabuse him of it. Or manage his expectations down as is so popular to do nowadays.

But I also don't live in la-la land.

There is a tactical side of love that goes hand-in-hand with the rapid heartbeat, the five-hour telephone conversation, the damp sheets that gather in your balled-up fist.

It was summed up best to me by a businessman, of all people. Not some poet. I met him on a train a few years ago and he was a funny, glad-hander type. He had some of his employees with him and was trying to keep things light as they traveled back and forth from his offices in Philly, New York, and Washington D.C.

I sat down with him and his crew on the Philly to D.C. leg of the trip—they actually made room for me as the train was packed. It was nice of them. I was exhausted and didn't relish the idea of standing for a few hours—especially as I'd already been camping out for weeks at the Children's Hospital of Philadelphia, where my youngest daughter had been born with every medical problem imaginable.

When the businessman noticed my hospital bracelet, he leaned in to me and asked, "How's your marriage?"

Very direct. Just like that.

"Great," I answered. "Otherwise you'd probably have to wrestle the gun out of my mouth."

He laughed. "You're blessed," he said.

I knew that.

"You know, my first marriage was a colossal disaster," he told me. "I mean, on a biblical scale." He went on to tell me about how bitter and angry that marriage had made him. That he'd vowed, as he was going through his horror-show divorce, to never, ever marry again.

"Can you believe it? I met my wife in the middle of all of this," he said. "It was flat-out love."

But his soon-to-be-ex-wife was suing the hell out of him, and their kids were a disaster. He felt both used and used up and was terrified at the prospect of getting it wrong again. Nor could he imagine, for the life of him, how someone could love a man who was going through what he was going through. And worse, who'd brought it upon himself.

"But you know what?" he said. "My wife was always part of the solution and never part of the problem."

That observation alone could describe every happy partnership I've ever known.

"A few years later," he continued, "we had a sick kid born at the same hospital where your daughter's being treated. I remember sitting outside on one of the benches and thanking God that this had happened with the woman I'm married to now and not my ex-wife. Otherwise I would've ended up on the nightly news."

He cupped his hand over mine and ran his finger over my hospital bracelet. "It's the most important decision you'll ever make—choosing your mate. It can make or break your life."

And don't those kinds of stakes deserve the sorts of over-the-top dreamy declarations we find so simple-minded in any self-respecting Once Upon A Time love story?

Why We Need to Laugh at Everything

I've often raised eyebrows among friends and strangers alike for my admittedly dark sense of humor. For me, nothing—and I really do mean that I can't think of a single thing—is off limits. Not racism, not poverty, not cancer, not Alzheimer's, not Nazis or Communists or Democrats or Republicans or religion—including my own Catholic faith.

I know that just the mention of these topics in anything but the most earnest, delicate voice leaves many aghast, and I definitely understand why there is a reflexive, negative reaction to what some call black humor and others simply call insensitive, politically incorrect humor.

But to me, black humor is deeply misunderstood.

I believe the hostility stimulated by farcical, often morbid jokes that make light of what are unquestionably very serious, painful subjects has to do with the misconception that the person making those jokes is somehow mocking the pain of a given people or situation. The imagined result is the further infliction of grief on an already damaged being—a child, a slave, a man born grossly disfigured, perhaps.

But in true black humor, the only mockery is of the absurd, the tyrannical, the sanctimonious. It's meant to slay the boogieman and allow nothing—not a hateful word or heartache—to hold power over an individual.

I was reminded of this when a friend of mine sent me a link from the *New York Times* that chronicled a new Czech reality TV series called *Holiday in the Protectorate*. In it, three generations of a real-life contemporary Czech family are sent "back in time" for a reality show reenactment of the German invasion of Czechoslovakia. The show's contestants are made to live in a remote area of the Czech Republic that was the first part of the country to be invaded and annexed by the Nazis at the onset of World War II.

There, according to the NYT feature, "They must not only survive the rigors of rustic life with outdated appliances and outdoor plumbing [circa late 1930s Czechoslovakia], but navigate the moral and physical dangers of life under Nazi rule." Some of these dangers include air raids, having their doors kicked down and property searched by the Gestapo (played by actors), being betrayed by snitches, and having to scavenge and traverse the black market in order to have enough food to simply keep from starving.

If they perform well, in everyday tasks such as cooking over a chalet stove and milking cows, as well as in life-and-death challenges such as managing not to get shot, they stand to win about forty grand.

Naturally, I was all over this. I immediately posted the link to the article on Facebook, writing, "Move over, Kardashians, this is my kind of reality show." To me, this much-maligned genre was finally taking on something of real, historical significance; a welcome antidote to the mere peeling back of the curtain on the lives of the shallow and pampered. I thanked my friend by name and within minutes received a note from her in the comment box saying, "I'm not endorsing it, Vic!"

In fact, not a single one of my 887 Facebook friends liked or commented on the article, except for my mother—a mischling who was actually born under the Nazi occupation, and whose parents concealed their own racial secret while hiding and smuggling Jewish friends.

But to everyone but my mom, the article was like Kryptonite.

And I can understand why. The show itself, while getting a lot of attention, has been denounced by critics around the globe as trivializing a "brutal and dehumanizing period." Much offense has centered around the title of the show, as Nazi rule was "no holiday."

The Czech director of the series, herself a very earnest woman in her thirties, by the looks of her, says she is surprised at not only the volume of attention her show has received, but the often sight-unseen condemnation. Couldn't people understand, she told the reporter, that the title was meant ironically? That the episodes, in and of themselves, were meant to educate modern viewers about a time in history, make it real for them in a way that also happens to entertain and keep their attention?

And this is the crux of black humor, is it not? The fact that through irony, juxtaposition, comedy, and yes, even amusement, we are able to look into, past, under, over and through the most agonizing, unimaginable events both in our lives and in the world at large.

Look, I know that my innate sense of the dark and the funny coming together like a Reese's peanut butter cup isn't for everyone. Much of it comes from my Czech culture, so it's no shock my people would come up with something like this: a Nazi-themed reality show that's darkly humorous in concept if not context and execution.

Of course, my husband shares my sensibility and he's

Irish, so this is not a trait specific to the Slav. But the Irish are no strangers to making light of an inherently awkward, gut-wrenching, or just plain ole bad luck set of circumstances either. (Anybody out there ever read Jonathan Swift's pitch-black masterpiece "A Modest Proposal"?)

And we're not the *can dish it out, but can't take it* type, either.

A few minutes after our infant daughter received her cancer diagnosis eight years ago—and on my birthday, no less—my husband and I were faced with even more bad news. In addition to the potentially deadly chemo, our daughter would require more surgery to assess her damaged liver. Basically, we were told, if the liver biopsy came back bad, she was dead. Somehow, without missing a beat, I turned to the doctor and said, "So let me get this straight. If the liver's okay, we get to try our luck in a gulag; but if it's not, a rusty iron ingot will be driven through our eyeballs?" My husband doubled over. What started as a snicker for me became an all-out crack-up. I was shaking, my eyes were tearing—I couldn't even look at my husband without dissolving into yet another fit of laughter.

Even our daughter's surgeon wasn't immune to the contagion. He held it together—barely—and said, "Well, that's one way of putting it." The good doctor was no stranger to gallows humor. He'd already heard worse—from us, no less—and deeply understood how badly we needed a laugh. We'd been dealing with our daughter's health problems since right about my second ultrasound in my fourth month of pregnancy and her birth had taken us to a new level of stress. And now, he was telling us, the stakes had just been raised once again. A knock-knock joke just wasn't going to cut it. The situation demanded a heinous and ballsy comparison to the pits of despair. It required unbridled insanity and a complete re-framing of our circumstances. Something that would carry us into the next day, or just the next hour. To help us even understand, for the love of God, what we were experiencing.

Because black humor, like prayer, takes some of the weight off. It can make us smarter about the real goings on—spiritual, political, metaphysical. It leads us into asking unorthodox questions and drawing unexpected conclusions.

Laughter, we forget, is also a teacher.

I always think of reading about when Robin Williams busted into Christopher Reeve's hospital room shortly after the Superman actor's devastating spinal cord injury. Disguised as a doctor and wearing an ear loop surgical mask, he began describing in cringe-inducing detail how he was about to perform an extensive and invasive rectal exam on his paralyzed friend.

Christopher Reeve credited that laugh with helping him want to live, and with giving him insight into his own reserves. That bit of tasteless humor showed him that joy was still possible—even if he would never hold his wife or children again, or feel the warmth of their skin and their hearts beating against his chest. He would not walk, run, make love, caress, tickle, or be tickled. But damn it, he would laugh. Laugh so hard that he couldn't catch his breath. Laugh until it was dangerous and his doctors had to intervene. And after he was done laughing, he would teach us all a little bit about what true resilience meant.

Only God Could Have Created Christopher Hitchens

There is but one man who could have lured me away from my husband. Even if just for a tawdry weekend of boozing, arguments, smoke-filled hotel rooms, and failed attempts at consummating some form of lust.

That man was Christopher Hitchens.

Hitch has been dead for four years and I still miss him. It wasn't an anniversary of his birth or death that made me get all *sniff* about him once again, it was picking up a copy of *Vanity Fair* at the gym.

Having not glanced through the magazine in at least a couple of years, I'd forgotten how little it has to offer now that Hitch is gone from its pages. Without him, *Vanity Fair* just depresses me. It's an empty Prada suit. A celebrity as light as cotton candy trying desperately to project gravitas.

For those of you who are a little fuzzy about who Christopher Hitchens was, I'll tell you a bit about him, then go on to tell you what he meant to me. To Wikipedia, he was "a British-American author, philosopher, polemicist, debater, and journalist. He contributed to *New Statesman, The Nation, The Atlantic, The London Review of Books, The Times Literary Supplement* and *Vanity Fair*."

To me, he was a contrarian, a true thinker, a heart-felt belly laugh, and bright spot in so many dreary days.

"The four most over-rated things in life are champagne, lobster, anal sex and picnics," he observed rightly.

Unlike other public intellectuals, who are most often pompous prigs who make you want to run for your life, Hitch was a good time. He looked like hell, drank as spiritedly as he argued, told great jokes and judged his fellow man only by merit and character. His friends said he made hipsters look needy.

Of course, his hard living killed him in the end, but even about that, he was unrepentant.

"In one way, I suppose, I have been 'in denial' for some time, knowingly burning the candle at both ends and finding that it often gives a lovely light," he said, after being diagnosed with esophageal cancer in 2010.

He told Charlie Rose in a subsequent television interview, "Writing is what's important to me, and anything that helps me do that — or enhances and prolongs and deepens and sometimes intensifies argument and conversation — is worth it to me," adding that it was "impossible for me to imagine having my life without going to those parties, without having those late nights, without that second bottle."

I realize a lot of people didn't like Hitch and weren't sorry to see him go—maybe not from life itself, but certainly from the public stage. The fact is, the man was contentious, self-important and never afraid to change his mind.

A passionate Marxist in his youth, he broke ranks with the Left for the first time when his dear friend, Booker Prize Winner Salman Rushdie, began receiving death threats after the publication of his novel, *The Satanic Verses*, in 1989. The book apparently offended certain Muslim clerics, including none other than the Ayatollah Khomeini, the Supreme Leader of Iran at the time. He sentenced Rushdie to death with a *fatwa*, and forced him into hiding.

The glitterati, Hitchens felt, were mealy-mouthed in support of their colleague.

"Utterly spineless," Hitchens would say.

For all of their posturing about human rights, when it came time for the Left to stand by their friend, Rushdie, they did not. Hitchens never forgave them.

"It was, if I can phrase it like this, a matter of everything I hated versus everything I loved," he wrote in his memoir, *Hitch-22*. "In the hate column: dictatorship, religion, stupidity, demagogy, censorship, bullying and intimidation. In the love column: literature, irony, humor, the individual and the defense of free expression."

But his hatred of Henry Kissinger, Margaret Thatcher, and Ronald Reagan kept him on the up-and-up with his friends at *The Nation*, even if they had to hold their noses after he publicly excoriated them for their cowardice on the Rushdie issue.

It wouldn't be until the September 11th attacks in 2001 that Hitchens would sever his ties with *The Nation*, and thus effectively the Left, for good. His enthusiastic and unwavering support of the wars in Iraq and Afghanistan was an unforgivable breach. Especially since—right or wrong—he could argue his conclusions better than anyone on either side of the debate.

But if you think he went running into the arms of the Right, think again. While hawkish in his desire to "fully destroy our enemies. I hate them. With a passion," he said, he was no friend of the Right. He despised religious fundamentalism and frankly, religion, on any level, and found the conservative movement's civil and women's rights legacy appalling. While he wrote an eloquent piece in *Slate* about why he did not regret George W. Bush's two turns in the White House, he also supported Obama in 2008.

"I don't envy or much respect people who are completely politicized," he said.

To the frustration of both his friends and enemies, Hitch switched sides with a kind of ruthlessness that indicated his attachment to thought, not ideas. And that's what I loved so much about him. He understood how crippled one was without the other. How ideas—no matter how great and important—are meant to be assailed by thought and assailed mercilessly. Ideas on politics, on sexuality, on science, on class, on race, and yes, on religion.

"I learned that very often the most intolerant and narrow-minded people are the ones who congratulate themselves on their tolerance and open-mindedness."—Christopher Hitchens

Ain't that the truth.

A Long Day's Journey Into Light

My switch from non-believer to believer has been more of a slow evolution than a short, sharp shock. You know the kind of "blinding light followed by the voice of Christ" conversion that St. Paul experienced on the road to Damascus?

Well, that's not me.

First of all, my conversation with God began at the gym. And it was definitely one-sided.

I was lifting a ten-pound weight, trying to beef up my left bicep, letting my mind run wild—thinking about the story I'd just begun writing, wondering whether I wanted to make roast chicken or lasagna for dinner, and plotting my next adventure with my husband. Childless and newly married, we had moved to San Francisco the previous year and were taking some sort of little road trip almost every weekend. Often, it was my job to dream them up.

As I switched the weight from my left to my right hand, it suddenly occurred to me that while I lived my exterior life with tremendous imagination—that very moment contemplating a visit to Bodega Bay, where Hitchcock's *The Birds* was filmed—I approached my spiritual life with the creative vision of a bureaucrat. Out of a combination of laziness, and frankly, smugness, I had stamped a big NO into the box for belief.

So, for the first time since my senior year in high school,

I cleared my throat and in my mind's voice said, "Hello, is anybody there?"

The simple answer was no.

But for some reason I didn't stop asking the question. Every few months or weeks, I would basically just say "hi, there," and wait to see what would happen. And, well, nothing happened.

It wasn't until some two years later when I actually decided to do something about my lame attempts at seeking God.

I was in a book store in the Castro district with my nearly eight-month-old son looking for a book of poetry to give a friend on his birthday. I hate choosing poetry for people—it's so personal, like picking out their underwear. But when you get it right, you're able to add something of real value to their lives. A thought, a metaphor, a validation of a buried dream that will travel with them always. I wanted to do that for this friend, but I was struggling.

"You should try William Carlos Williams," a man next to me said, handing me a copy of his collected poems.

"It's for a friend," I said, casually flipping through the book. I'd never read William Carlos Williams and for some reason didn't want to.

"They're wonderful poems," the man said with genuine emotion. He looked at my young son. "I'm a Catholic priest. Would you mind if I blessed your son?"

I should mention at this point that my husband and I had left the Catholic Church in a huff, separately, during our college years. We were angry with their treatment of women, their refusal to sanction birth control in even the most poverty-stricken countries, and their over-all "holier than thou" attitude about everything. Our marriage was a civil ceremony as we had no intention of going through the required Pre Cana (basically premarital couples counseling officiated by a priest) that precipitates any Catholic marriage, and we had recently been congratulating ourselves for having left the Church, given the pedophilia scandal it was embroiled in at the time.

We did want to give our son some spiritual grounding, however, and had looked into Buddhism (we're not groovy enough), Judaism (we're only a quarter Jewish, each), and the Unitarian Church (too Protestant).

Anyway, I looked at this Catholic priest standing next to me—dressed in a sweater, a raincoat, jeans and a fedora—and he seemed nice. And I'd let a transsexual healer fresh from an all-nighter bless my pregnant belly some months back, so why not a poetry-loving priest?

"Sure," I said. He asked me my son's name.

"Eamon Francis Dougherty."

"Oh, you're Catholic!"

Busted.

"Mmm-hmm."

"Where do you go to church?"

"Um, we're kind of new to San Francisco," I explained. "We're still looking."

"How long have you been here?" he asked.

I felt like a little kid again. "Actually, three years."

He didn't judge and he didn't miss a beat.

"You must try St. Gabriel's," the priest told me. "You'll love it. The nine o'clock mass is perfect for children, really any mass there is, but that's the one families most attend."

To make a long story a little less long, I strode through my front door with a book of poems by William Carlos Williams stuffed into my armpit and told my husband, "We're going to church on Sunday." Regardless of recent meanderings, he knew exactly what I meant by "church."

"Just go with me on this."

"Okay," he said.

I wish I could remember the homily on that next Sunday when we attended mass at St. Gabriel's, but I can't. I only know that it was soulful, beautiful, relevant and utterly down to earth at the same time. I do remember the priest saying in a pronounced Irish brogue, "There's a lot of noise here today—giggling and whispering from the children. Crying. And I want you all to know that if this is bothering you, I'm afraid you're at the wrong church."

For the first time in our entire lives, although we'd attended years of Catholic school and hundreds of masses, my husband and I had a moving experience during a service.

We became regulars at St. Gabriel's, even if we couldn't quite call ourselves believers yet. That would come a long way down the road. But we made friends with the man I'd met at the book shop—Father John. Shortly after my son's first birthday, we did what we'd sworn we'd never do: we had him baptized in the Catholic Church.

When Father John sprinkled holy water on Eamon's still-bald head during the ceremony, he said, "Eamon Francis Dougherty, you are a poet, a priest and a king." My husband's eyes welled up. He still says that to our son every night before we head off to bed—even though the boy is nearly thirteen.

It would be years before I would hear anything even resembling an answer to the tentative greeting I offered God at my gym. Before I could call myself a Catholic with a straight face, to be perfectly honest. Or even a believer in anything other than strong values, love, and good citizenship.

I would be at the Children's Hospital of Philadelphia in

a grieving room that was offered to me while my new baby underwent a life or death surgery—one of several she'd already been through, but this time I felt at the end of my rope.

I was rolled up in fetal position on a cot and my hands were folded together so tightly that my fingers had gone numb. In the morning, when the nurse came to get me, I would actually have trouble prying them apart.

But that night, I finally heard something. And no, it wasn't a voice. I guess it was more a feeling than a sound. It was what I can only describe as the heartbeat of the universe. It was a notion, a hunch, an impression—I don't know—but one that without saying a word told me that I was a part of it and that no matter what the outcome of my daughter's surgery would be, my family was safe.

I didn't spring into that next day with all of my problems solved. Nor were the next few years a breeze because I'd had this experience. But I did feel different. I felt stronger and like anything was possible. And by that, I mean even the worst I could possibly imagine.

And I understood, for the first time, what it meant—doubtlessly, categorically—to love.

On Love and Forgiveness

A Story of Two People Who Screwed Up Royally and in the End Got it So Right

I ran into a friend of mine at the gym the other day.

On her face was a configuration of emotions—serenity, wistfulness, sorrow. She had an end-of-the-road look about her.

"One of my best friends is dying of cancer," she said. "It could be any time now."

I told her how sorry I was, and she sort of smiled and went on to tell me, truly, one of the loveliest stories I've heard in a long, long time.

This friend of my friend's—we'll call her Marilyn—had several years ago been embroiled in a horrible divorce. She and her husband, whom we'll call Jake, had cheated on each other, called one another every possible, filthy name in the book, had fought over their bedroom furniture, collection of DVDs, even all the family photos they'd collected throughout their marriage. It was brutal and ugly and they were both at fault. They let down themselves and their children—a pitiful end to a union that had undoubtedly begun with the ambitious, heart-stopping words most of us married people spoke at our weddings: "With this ring I thee wed, with my body I thee worship, and with all my worldly goods I thee endow."

Even when the divorce was finalized, and the anger had begun to subside, it seemed all that remained of that original promise was shame and bitterness.

A couple of years after the dust from their split had settled, Marilyn was diagnosed with breast cancer and underwent treatment. She was hopeful that would be the end of it, and set about going on with her life—sweating through spinning classes at our gym, driving carpool for her daughters. But three years later, she received her worst and final diagnosis—that of terminal ovarian cancer. This friend, daughter, and mother of two teenage girls had only months to live.

At this point you might be asking, "Isn't this supposed to be a lovely story?"

But wait! Don't quit reading now. I acknowledge that was the horrible part. The park your lawn chair on the railroad tracks, pop a cold beer and wait for the inevitable portion of this saga.

The lovely part—no, lovely doesn't even begin to cut it. The magnificent part, the miraculous part, came in the immediate aftermath of Marilyn's diagnosis. When she called Jake, her ex-husband, and told him the news.

I'll just cut to the chase here, because Marilyn and Jake did exactly that. What happened next was that Marilyn and Jake fell in love again. And not just in a friendly, hand-holding, I'm really sorry you're going to die way, but a balls-out, heart wanting to explode, Harlequin romance, listen to Lionel Ritchie records together and cry kind of way.

Jake took over all correspondence about Marilyn's condition—sharing bits of news with friends and family members, asking for prayers. He whisked her away to fancy dinners, shuttled her to doctors' appointments, guided her on long walks, helped her to the toilet.

Her illness has progressed pretty rapidly since those early months and Marilyn has become frail. Jake now brushes her hair and reads to her. He pushes her wheelchair to their daughters' games, and has moved into hospice with her—holding her all night.

"Are you sure you didn't make all this cancer stuff up just to get laid?" one of Marilyn's friends joked.

And days ago, Jake surprised Marilyn with a trip to the oak tree under which they were married. He had to carry her, as Marilyn is down to only about sixty pounds now. She can no longer eat and is basically starving to death.

Under that oak tree, Jake and Marilyn renewed their vows. "To have and to hold from this day forward, for better for worse, for richer for poorer, in sickness and in health, to love and to cherish, till death us do part."

"They just forgave each other," my gym buddy told me. "It's as simple as that."

Marilyn's illness brought everything into relief for them. The fact that they'd been crazy about each other once and then proceeded to screw up massively. Anger had replaced love, and even when they'd wanted make up, take back the terrible things they'd said and done, it felt too big. Like they'd gone too far down a very dark road and there was no going back.

Only there was.

And when they did go back, it was instant, sublime—a bolt of lightning illuminating the night sky. They needed no couples' therapy or promises to never hurt one another again. They simply didn't have time for that.

"You know what this has taught me?" my friend said. "None of us have time for that."

It's a radical statement. Aren't we, according to the experts, supposed to examine our feelings, work our way to acceptance and forgiveness, negotiate the new terms of our bandaged relationship?

Seems like a colossal waste of time when you look at it. Isn't the nature of forgiveness to let go completely—put it behind you and embrace the love that's left. Build on that, do it right. We all know what right looks like, feels like, what it should be. It's as plain as delighting in the flavors of a favorite dish, taking in the boundless glory of an ocean view. And we know damned well the pitfalls we need to avoid. We can name them like state capitols: jealousy, selfishness, entitlement, neglect.

Don't misunderstand me here. I'm not saying we should welcome back a spouse who thrives on slapping us around or a friend whose betrayal cost us dearly. One who shows no sign of remorse or change. Being a doormat is not what forgiveness is about.

Sometimes forgiveness is just about letting go and moving on alone. Wishing someone no ill, even if they're still a son of a bitch and will probably always be a son of a bitch.

But I do think we can all learn a few things from Marilyn and Jake's extraordinary love story. Even if we're not facing a death sentence. Instead of patching things up, they opted to start fresh. They made a conscious decision to love one another regardless of the mess they'd made of things years earlier, and in the process gave their girls and each other a most unequivocal gift. Something few of us are able to achieve.

Forgiveness with no footnotes, no terms.

Love, pure and simple.

[the ultimate expression]

A Case For Sorrow-Loveliness

Years ago, when my husband decided to treat himself to a trip to Auschwitz for his thirtieth birthday, it raised a lot of eyebrows. I mean, really, why not Vegas? But I got it. His father had recently died, and being of Irish-Jewish decent, he felt a certain draw. I'm especially fond of that particular trip of his to Eastern Europe because we met there—in Prague, at a 300-year-old candle-lit pub just two days before he left for his tour of the Nazi death camp.

Months later, when we were already in love, he told me about his experience.

He said, like many people I know who've visited, that the Auschwitz part of the complex wasn't as compelling as he'd thought it would be. It consisted mostly of plain brick buildings that could've been anything. There was something sanitized about it that he couldn't quite put his finger on.

The part of the complex that really hit him in the gut was Birkenau. Birkenau is where the "surviving" inmates lived—the ones who weren't gassed upon arrival. In bunkers built on a barren field. Somewhere behind that field, there's a small body of water called the Pond of Ashes, and even then, more than sixty years later, it was still a murky gray from the cinders of burnt corpses.

It's a place of unbearable sorrow beget by unspeakable

cruelty and yet my husband told me about standing at that pond and watching a bevy of deer trot by as if they lived in the most glorious place on Earth. This was their home, and they shared it unreservedly with the souls of the departed. He said that if they were able, the deer would've smiled at him.

Maybe the deer were indifferent to human suffering and only saw the beauty of their home: The mist in the trees and the cawing of black birds, the comic melody of the Polish language spoken throughout the countryside.

Or maybe they found a tender allure in the vague smell of death that still clings to the landscape even though it's been decades since a smoke smelling of burnt cashews rose from the chimney stalks. It could be the melody of the visitors' sobs and not the inhabitants' chatter that makes this place home.

"*Ponurý*," I said, and my husband gave me a quizzical look. He'd never heard of what would become his favorite word.

If you look up *ponurý* in an English-Czech dictionary, it will be defined as gaunt, gloomy, dismal and grim, but that's not its only definition. The way I've understood *ponurý* is more nuanced. To my Czech friend, Katerina, it means "sorrow-lovely," implying the beauty in pain, the soulful, life-affirming misery of a stormy day.

"Ah," my husband said. I'd been able put my finger on something that he'd always recognized, but as an American had no way to define. To Americans, sorrow equals one thing—bad. Ain't no lovely about it.

Ponurý. I can't imagine a place like Auschwitz-Birkenau conjuring any other feeling. My experience of the place, I told my husband, wasn't all that different from his. It involved wrapping my brain around an almost crushing sense of tragedy—yes—but was also filled with tranquility, camaraderie, and even comedy.

I first went to Auschwitz almost two years to the day before my husband visited and had his deer sighting. I was a translator for a British film crew that was making a documentary on the Czech composer Pavel Haas, who died there.

The Prague we'd left was in vivid color, and the train we'd boarded was more muted—flecked with reds and golds, dirty browns, and dulled French blues. It was a creaky, communist train—each car still stamped with a prominent red star, though it was 1993. We headed for Poland from Prague on a night that looked a lot like it belonged in Casablanca—the movie, not the Moroccan city. The moon was full, but covered by a thin wisp of clouds that seemed almost like a piece of white muslin wrapped around a fat auntie's belly. The night was wet cold and our fellow passengers were mostly Polish gypsies, each of whom looked easily ten years older than they were and swore with a gusto I'd never encountered before. They threw the word "cunt" around as if it were no different than "dude" and could spit out an insult more grotesque than a hard, wet lugie. They lived close to the death camp complex, but appeared to have no interest in it—even if countless of their people, perhaps even members of their own family, had perished there.

I didn't know my British companions very well. They were BBC journalists with a cameraman and a producer thrown in for good measure. All of them pleasant and smart. I remember doing shots with them in the bar car, but what really stood out about that night—other than the moon—was the way one of the gypsies called me a "stinkin' cock-sucking cunt of a dead, rotting bitch" for not telling her I was American. She'd been fooled by my then-flawless Czech and knew she'd missed a big opportunity when the border guard demanded our passports and I whipped out a dark blue little booklet with *the United States of America* printed in gold on its cover. Had she known, she would've hidden her contraband in my suitcase. "They never check the Americans," she told me. And it's true—half her suitcase was confiscated and they never even peeked in mine. That night, I slept with my money and passport shoved into my underwear like a maxi pad.

The journalists thought that was hilarious.

I figured by the time we stepped off the platform in Oswiecim (as Auschwitz is called in Polish), I would be entering a black and white film. But I didn't. Even though it was an overcast day that saw some drizzle in the afternoon, the air was refreshing, and the death camp complex was clean and unassuming. I remember someone had written into the dust on one of the sleeping bunks, "Let he who has never discriminated cast the first stone." I thought—big difference between discriminate and exterminate, buddy—whoever you are. And that's when I saw it—my equivalent of the deer by the ash pond. Beyond the fence that encloses the complex was a cluster of small houses. I watched a woman in a housedress amble outside carrying a bundle of wet dish rags. One by one, she hung them on a clothes line. I heard a voice in the distance and the woman waved—a neighbor had come home. She hardly seemed to notice us and we couldn't have been more than fifty feet away.

"How can anyone live here?" someone said from behind me. Maybe it was the camera man. If I'd known then about the deer, I would've told him. I might have said something as simple as "It's their home." Or, if he'd seemed eager to listen, and I was willing to talk, I might've told him about *ponurý*, and the counter-intuitive enchantment it can cast over an unsuspecting soul.

Truth, Beer, and History's Massive Tailwind

In 1995 I had the good fortune to accompany a Czech film crew to a celebration commemorating the fiftieth anniversary of the liberation of the city of Pilsen, Czech Republic by us Americans.

It was a joyous event filled with music, great beer (it is the town of Pilsen, after all, where the name Pilsner comes from), hearty food (dumplings, anyone?), and scores of veterans from all the world over. Freedom was new to that part of the world, and it still felt like a dream. The way it must feel in the aftermath of winning the lottery.

About an hour into the merriment, parade watching, and copious beer drinking, I realized that if I didn't find a bathroom, things might get ugly.

I ran into what I thought was a welcome center and was immediately pointed in the direction of a clean, unisex toilet by a kindly woman manning a beer tap.

When I emerged, I figured I could use another beer, so I went over to the woman at the tap and started digging some coins out of my pocket.

"No, no," she said, and handed me the beer free of charge. "Sit down."

She offered me a platter studded with several rows of *topinky*, which is basically the Czech version of bruschetta:

slices of rye bread fried in lard, spread with a thick layer of lard (think cream cheese on a bagel), and topped with diced raw onions and a sprinkle of salt and paprika.

"You're American, so you're used to the truth," she said between bites of *topinky*. She pointed outside at the celebration. "But for us, you can see it's still a luxury."

And that's when she told me her story.

It so happened that of the American troops that liberated Pilsen, at least one was an African-American regiment. In the wild revelry that lasted for days after the citizens of Pilsen were finally freed from the Nazis . . . well, let's just say there were a lot of very grateful Czech women and a lot of handsome men in uniform around. Not to mention fountains of really great beer to fuel the fire. My new beer wench friend happened to be one of those grateful women, and about nine months after the partying died down, she gave birth to a beautiful, brown baby boy.

Now, what was then Czechoslovakia didn't have the same kind of racial baggage that we had over here in the United States. People of color (unless you were a Romani) really were just that, and garnered stares only because they were exotic. So, while an unwed mother was still a bit of a scandal back in the mid-to-late 1940s, the fact that the child was dark-skinned was neither here nor there.

Except for one little problem.

Once the Soviets took over the country, they took over the country's history as well and declared that it was in fact the Russians—not the Americans—who liberated Pilsen. Contradicting this new truth carried some pretty heavy consequences, which left my new friend in a pickle: fair-skinned babies could be explained away easily, but the dark ones gave new meaning to the ethnic term "Black Russian."

"So, what happened?" I asked.

"At first I was scared they might take my son. You know, disappear him," she said. "But it was funny. Instead, people started to pretend he looked like everyone else. I met my husband a couple of years after the war and people would go out of their way to tell me how much my dark son looked like my husband and our other children. Even people who knew. It was crazy. Without talking about it, everyone began to lie."

She started to wonder if she had imagined making love to an African American soldier and pondered other reasons that could explain her son's skin color. Maybe her child had inherited a recessive gene?

"At times," she said. "I really thought I was going crazy. Even my husband started going along with it."

One thing kept her sanity.

She was walking in the market with her son the first time it happened. He was little—maybe four or five—and right in front of her at a fruit stall, she spied a little boy just like hers: the same age, the same color. The other boy's mother saw them, too.

"What did you do?" I asked her.

"Nothing."

She told me that she and the other mother smiled at each other and went their separate ways. It was too dangerous for them to start talking. What they could say would only bring trouble.

And that wasn't the only mother she encountered over the years. There were a good handful in Pilsen, and when they saw each other on the street, they always smiled the satisfied smile of someone who knows the truth. Not only was it proof positive that they weren't crazy, but also a reminder that they were being ruled by lies and that there really was a better life out there. A life without fear, invented histories, and hopelessness. She told me she was very proud that the father of her child was American.

I guess it's one of history's little ironies that a dark-skinned boy was a symbol of truth and hope in a totalitarian society, and one of oppression and bitterness left over from a civil war and a slave trade in a free one. I didn't have the heart to tell her that her son's father went home to a segregated society.

But I did have the heart to tell her what I know to be true: that as long as people are free to speak, things can change quickly. Lies are contradicted. Subject to a constant stream of information, bad policies are over-turned, and even hearts and minds evolve.

The Bone Church: Real and Imagined

The Ossuary at Sedlec—or Bone Church of Kutna Hora, as it's more commonly known—is a relatively plain church from the exterior. At least as far as Old World European standards go. It sits about an hour outside of Prague in the Czech Republic, and last time I was there, some ten years ago, it was still a dingy mustard color on the outside.

In fairness, most ossuaries are just church basements filled with neatly piled-up human bones, so there typically isn't anything out of the ordinary about the actual structure it's housed in. There's no electrically powered Grim Reaper standing with a scythe and chuckling a deep *mwaahhaahaaa*, the way there is at any self-respecting haunted house.

In fact, the only feature that advertised there just might be more than meets the eye to the Bone Church of Kutna Hora was the skull and crossbones spiked at the top of its spire—right where you'd usually see a crucifix.

Otherwise, the place just sat there like Boris Karloff without make-up.

When I visited on a gloomy October day in 2004, dragging my twenty-month-old son and a prehistoric digital camera with me, I thought I would have to muscle my way through a throng of tourists.

But we were alone.

Suitably, the only sounds we could hear were my own boot heels clicking on the stone tiles as we entered the foyer, the wheels of my son's dilapidated MacLaren stroller, and the whistle of a fall wind—the kind that blows tufts of dead leaves in a swirl. Some of those, mostly a fresh cluster of fiery orange oak leaves, blew with us into the Bone Church. A young man, very pale and black haired with a warm smile and crooked teeth, greeted us.

It should have been eerie, but it was exquisite.

A short staircase—also stone—led us down into the chamber, where an enormous chandelier lorded over the place. It was fashioned entirely of human bone—utilizing every bone in the human body, the young man told us in his hushed, churchy voice. The skulls would have held candles, I suppose, but the chandelier was unlit. In fact, the only light in the Bone Church came from the outside through a few kidney-shaped Gothic windows.

There were urns made primarily of femurs, a bone coat of arms belonging to the Schwarzenberg family, an endless garland (skull-vertebrae-vertebrae-knee cap, skull-tibia-skull-tibia) strung loosely along the trim like it was Christmas and several pyramids constructed of bones—ones that sat in iron-barred enclaves like slayed prisoners.

My son and I stood there absorbing the sheer magnitude of death around us. People who'd died of flu, arsenic poisoning, small pox, swords thrust into their rib cage, a heart attack, a mallet to the temple, infection, childbirth, trampling, a broken heart.

The bones of some thirty thousand Christians beautified this stark, chapel-like holy chamber—prominent and presumably pious Christians who had been promised burial in the Church of All Saints cemetery. But due to a string of plagues and wars, had found themselves without a place to land after they blew their last breath.

It occurred to me this strange permanent installation of sacred art—the devil's art, some called it—was actually a clever solution to a very sensitive dilemma. Church teachings, after all, forbade cremation at the time. And the poor souls who had counted on burial in the Church of All Saints holy cemetery had paid considerable tithes to earn their way into some kind of dignified and noble entombment.

And what could be more noble than the care and inspired vision required to create such a communal, yet deeply personal way to honor the departed? To me, it was the ultimate expression of both grief and hope.

My little son—and my first and most tender reminder of my own mortality—was getting restless and hungry, so I snapped a couple of pictures and we left.

But the Bone Church stayed with me and made its way into a story I'd begun writing.

[when we dance]

State of Grace

A Short Explanation Of A (Former) Atheist's Faith

Historically, I have not been a person faith comes easily to. I am a rational science geek—albeit with a serious artistic stripe—who feels about Carl Sagan the way a lot of people feel about John Lennon.

I have to wake up every day and make a concerted effort to discover God as if I've found Him for the first time. Some people have experienced few blessings and have perhaps seen no evidence of miracles in their lives, yet they believe with an unwavering passion. As for me, I've had blessing upon blessing, been the recipient of Divine Providence, Divine Intervention and of miracles large and small. Yet it is a struggle for me to believe.

It is my single greatest failure of imagination.

Despite my meager faith, every prayer I have ever uttered—whether it was to the Catholic God of my youth, or to a god (or goddess) borrowed from another religion, or to "the universe," has been answered.

Given that kind of track record, when I first folded my hands nine years ago and reached out to God—not "the universe"—and asked Him if He could bestow upon me the blessing of faith—I felt a certain degree of confidence that whoever, whatever God was, He was listening.

Even if I'd closed my mind to Him for so long.

And having a pretty good grasp of Scripture after umpteen years of Catholic school, I knew God wasn't going to deliver faith on a silver platter just because I made the ask. Any more than He would deliver fame and fortune to a garage band that got high all day and never played an actual gig.

This was going to hurt.

But for some crazy reason, even though I really, really don't like pain—especially the emotional kind—I couldn't bring myself to take back my appeal for faith.

Faith had always gnawed at me—even when I was at the apex of my "rational period," as an atheist who delighted in boring the snot out of people with my backhanded insults about religion and intellect. Mainly how they don't go together.

And being a great lover of all things science, I just couldn't let that little, gnawing feeling go. I had to investigate. Even it killed me. Or at the very least, embarrassed me.

If you've read the previous essays in this volume, you probably know that I had a kid born with cancer a few years ago. And yes, of course that was the inciting incident for my current, rather devout faith in God.

But not for the reason you might think.

However flawed, mine is not a foxhole faith (as in "there are no atheists in a foxhole"). I'd be lying if I said I never prayed for my sick baby's recovery. For her to have a chance at a normal, happy life, and for me to get a chance to know her and love her. But I really didn't pray for that very often when she was sick.

What I prayed for was strength. And I got it. I also prayed for a deeper understanding of my own weird, sometimes tenuous faith. I got that, too.

I suppose the strongest testament to my faith is that I don't believe in God because he spared my daughter and I get to bask in the joy of hearing her laughter on any given day, and do her hair in the morning, and help her learn to spell. I would have been lucky to have known her at all—for however brief a period. Strangely, I would have been thankful to God for the experience of her death, too, however insane that might sound to a rationalist. It even sounds insane to me.

The increasing depth of my belief can be explained with mystical clarity in the eulogy from one of my favorite movies, *Pan's Labyrinth*.

"The essence of God's forgiveness lies in His word and in His mystery. Because although God sends us the message, it is our task to decipher it. Because when we open our arms, the earth takes in only a hollow and senseless shell. Far away now is the soul in its eternal glory. Because it is in pain that we find the meaning of life and the state of grace that we lose when we are born. Because God in his infinite wisdom puts the solution in our hands. And because it is only in his physical presence that the place he occupies in our souls is reaffirmed."

My rationale for belief can be explained with non-mystical clarity in my own words:

I believe in God because I believe in love.

Faith's Little Deaths

My husband, Jack, can be found on any given holiday entertaining my family with his over-the-top renditions of some of our Slavic tales of woe.

"Tell me, Jack, what you think is better?" he'll say in my grandmother's languorous accent. "To have your legs torn off in gulag and die like dog in ditch like Uncle Vladislavomiroslav? Or be burned alive slowly by laughing German soldiers like cousin Jiroslavomiravova?" Far from being offended, my mother will laugh until tears smear her thick mascara. My grandmother—smoke curling from her bottom lip—will wave her 120 cigarette and say, "Oh, you!"

Or at least she used to, God rest her soul.

It's easier to laugh about the big tragedies sometimes— the ones cartoonish in their proportions.

I know Jack and I had some of our heartiest, clutching our sides and nearly falling to the floor laughs when our youngest daughter, Josephine, was really, really sick. Especially when we didn't know if she would live or die. Laughs like that lighten the load and help keep you in love despite the storm raging around you.

Although I've laughed like a hyena at things like biliary atresia (or biliary atrocious, as we started calling it when Josephine was—wrongly, thank God—diagnosed with this condition), and all manner of afflictions and possible syndromes, I still can't laugh about a nurse I'll call Tatiana.

She was the nurse who neglected to feed my sick daughter through her feeding tube before heading off to her own cozy lunch. The same nurse who I overheard on the phone telling one of her friends that she thought she was too good for her job. That perhaps medical school was where she belonged.

I remember thinking *you are so wrong*. Trust me, as the daughter of not just a good, but a great doctor, medical school is not where you belong, girlfriend. And nursing, on the contrary, is way too good for you.

She performed her job with a boredom that bordered on contempt, and I detested listening to the way she would sigh when she actually had to get up off her bony ass and do something.

To this day, if I saw this nurse on the street my stomach would churn and my fists would clench in rage. I'm sure my face would contort into a mask of scorn and this young woman—who probably wouldn't even remember me—might say, "What's your problem, lady?"

You might think I'm overreacting. It was just a little vial of baby formula and it's not like my kid didn't get fed eventually.

She didn't starve.

But it was so much more than that. In that moment, under those circumstances, blowing off Josephine's feeding was not only careless, but cruel. My baby was doped up on morphine, hooked up to all sorts of machines, fighting for her life, and I wasn't even allowed to hold and comfort her. The only good thing in her whole existence right then was that her little tummy was getting filled on a regular basis and she didn't have to lie there being both hungry and in pain.

Honestly, in my mind, this nurse was on par with Hitler

and Stalin. And that's saying something. I shudder to think this careless, selfish brat ever went on to medical school. To this day, I hate the idea of her caring for patients in any capacity. I wonder what else she's forgotten to do, and if she was smart enough to cover it up. I know she thought she was.

In those situations—the *big* situations that come up in life sooner or later—it's the little deaths that can be hard to have a sense of humor about. The ones that reveal an ugly side of human nature instead of merely a case of bum luck—no matter how bum that luck turns out to be.

My mother, a Czech political refugee, will tell a story over and over again of a little girl she was teaching how to knit after school. I think my mom was about twelve or thirteen and the girl was a couple of years younger.

At that time, my mom didn't have a lot of friends. Given her political situation, most of the other kids treated her like toxic sludge.

And she loved hanging out with this girl, getting a chance to share a laugh, and treat her like a little sister. Knit one, pearl two.

Turned out the girl was reporting everything my mother said, or didn't say, to the local authorities for a few coins.

My mom was devastated when she found out, and even though she's had so many worse things happen to her in her life—she remembers in technicolor how she felt about this betrayal. Not even her abusive first marriage can evoke the kind of sadness that this little friend of hers can arouse to this day.

All of those hours they spent together. And none of them were real.

These are faith's little deaths.

They can happen anywhere, and don't have to be

accompanied by the fog of Nazis and the pollution of Communists. Or the horror and helplessness of watching someone you love suffer.

It may be, in fact, the more ambiguous tragedies that are the most devastating. They can ripple slowly through time like a single raindrop in placid waters.

They can be sneaky. Darkening our hearts, even in good times.

I know, for instance, that my daughter's illness feels increasingly like a distant memory to me. Even if she has had a few hiccups since the end of her treatment—a couple of surgeries and the occasional hospitalization. Those times come, but then go with a gigantic sigh of relief. She is eight years old, joyful and healthy. Things couldn't be better.

But Tatiana remains.

I feel her gaze in the odd mother who is uncomfortable with her daughter playing with Josephine because she knows in vague terms about our daughter's health problems. Even if Josephine appears every bit the normal child and requires no special attention. Even if the girls have been begging for a playdate with one another and I'm running out of excuses.

I sense Tatiana's indifference in every birthday party Josephine is not invited to.

I hate being so petty—cataloging slights and marking every missed occasion. After all, my daughter is oblivious and plays on with those of her friends whose mothers love having her over.

And I know I should just let it go. I recognize how toxic it is that I texted my husband with a snarky "Guess who just said hello with a big, fake smile and has an awful new hair color?" message during a field trip outing.

Not my shining moment.

But then last week, my daughter and I gave a presentation to her classmates about her illness and recovery. We did so at her teacher's suggestion because some of the kids had been wondering why Josephine has her own special bathroom to use. Stuff like that.

"They can handle it," Josephine's teacher told me. "They're compassionate kids and I think they'll find it interesting."

And they did. My little girl's classmates were fascinated by the rarity of her condition, and that she'd made the cover of her hospital's annual report because she was the child who that year had been treated by the most departments. They ran their fingers over the seemingly endless list of doctors, nurses and technicians who had cared for Josephine at one time or another. They were impressed by my daughter's pluck and shared their own ailments—allergies, a really, really bad cold once, a broken wrist, a twisted ankle, diabetes. That little friend of hers—the one she can't play with—cheered her on.

The weekend after our little presentation, I had to go out of town. On my way home, I got a text from my husband.

"Guess who's come over for a playdate?" he wrote and posted a picture of Josephine with her once forbidden friend. They seemed to be having a ball.

"I can't believe it," I texted back.

The next time I saw the mother, I smiled at her genuinely and we actually talked. She told me how much fun her daughter had at our house and that we have to do it again.

"Jo would love that," I said.

It felt good to open my heart to this woman again. To understand that maybe her reticence came out of fear and ignorance and we're all guilty of that at one time or another. It felt good to let go of my grudge and start fresh—leave that bit of baggage behind me. Hopefully for good. And stop the ripple that makes me question people's motives; sit in irate judgment of their seeming lack of compassion.

Perhaps revive some of my faith after all.

Greed, Envy And The Berlin Wall

On August 13 1961, the German Democratic Republic—otherwise known as Communist East Germany—began erecting a wall that would not only separate West Berlin from East Berlin—now known as just Berlin—but would effectively cut off West Berlin from its home in East Germany.

The Wall was barbaric, senseless, downright stupid, and a brazen lie, meant ostensibly to "protect its population from fascist elements conspiring to prevent the 'will of the people' in building a socialist state in East Germany." In reality, it was built to stop the mass defections of mostly young, talented, and educated Germans from an increasingly Sovietized government.

The Berlin Wall also included one of the most appalling symbols of the Cold War (apart from The Wall itself): a series of sniper-outfitted guard towers perched over a large area that became known as "the death strip." Need I even elaborate?

I visited Berlin shortly after the Wall was torn down in 1990, and I found the newly reunified city to be a living monument to the supremacy of free minds and free markets. East Berlin had the sorry look of good times past. It was dull and depressed, unkempt and uncared-for. Envy hung in the air like the stench of a dead possum.

Because then, just a few blocks away—visible,

accessible—was merry, glitzed-up, bustling West Berlin. Every day, the East Berliners got to gape at what they had missed, what they had been robbed of, and you could see that despite the joy of reunification it was killing them.

I think it would kill me, too.

Envy was one of the more insidious attributes of the East Bloc. True, Western, capitalist societies have greed—also, deservedly, one of the seven deadly sins. Greed is ugly and mean.

But I'll take greed over envy any time.

You may disagree with me and have many great reasons why I'm simply wrong, wrong, wrong, and I won't fight you with a tit for tat.

What I will do is tell you a joke.

A Czech (i.e. Communist), an American (i.e. Capitalist) and a Frenchman (we won't even go there) were sitting in a café and uncorked a bottle of wine. Lo and behold a genie popped out of the bottle and offered them each a wish in return for freeing him.

The American said, "Oh, me first, me first!"

The genie nodded for him to go ahead, since Americans always want to go first. And the American told him, "My neighbor has the most beeeaaauuutiful Cadillac I've ever seen. It's big, it's gold, and it's a convertible!"

The genie says, "So, you want that Cadillac."

"Heck no!" The American rubbed his hands together. "I want an even bigger, more beeeeautiful Cadillac."

His wish was granted.

Next, it was the Frenchman's turn. The Frenchman turned to the genie and said, "My neighbor has the most magnifique chateau! It is enormous! It has silver trim and gargoyles! The furniture is exquisite!"

"And you want that chateau?" the genie confirmed.

"But, of course!" The Frenchman said. "Only I want gold trim, bigger gargoyles and better furniture."

His wish was granted.

Finally, the Czech stepped forward. He took off his hat and bowed his head. "Mr. Genie," he said humbly. "My neighbor has the fattest, most succulent pig I have ever seen."

"Let me guess," the genie said. "You want an even fatter, more succulent pig."

"No," said the Czech. "I want that pig to die."

August In The Cold

Growing up Czech, I knew that Europeans had a different notion of how to spend a summer vacation than their American counterparts. Central and Eastern Europeans even more so.

It's not that Czechs and other East-ish Euros don't go on the same vacations we Americans go on—Disneyworld etc. It's more that they have a different notion of what summer is all about.

There is a "back to nature" quality to the warm months. A stripping down from the complexities of modern life that manifests itself in a total re-imagining of simple living.

It's about running around naked as much as possible. And bathing in the sea or any other body of water that is not a bathtub. Why open the tap when there's a "natural" water source around? Spelunking, climbing trees, chewing on onion grass straight out of the ground and picking wild berries and mushrooms—especially mushrooms. Cooking your own meals, wherever you are. Even if you're in France or Italy, where they will do it decidedly better than you ever could.

Lakes are a very big deal, particularly on weekends.

My Czech uncle will strip naked and dive into any old lake he happens to come across—even dubious ones just off the highway that might have signs reading "No Swimming."

He's suffered insults—"Hey, asshole, what are you

doing?", warnings, "Sir, you're not actually going to swim in there are you?", and directives "Put some clothes on, there are children present!" Not to mention him having been escorted away from many a body of water by our friends in uniform.

But that's never deterred him.

"It's hot! What is the water there for if not to swim?" he says. And he's got a point.

Some years ago, when my husband and I were visiting Prague together, he caught a glimpse of a tiny RV with a big sign posted onto the rear bumper. It read in German, "Hotel betten? Nein danke!" [Translation: Hotel bed? No, thank you!]

"What's that about?" he asked.

I went on to explain to him that refusing a nice, comfortable hotel was often not a matter of thrift, but ideology. We have all year to get all too comfortable in our pimped-up lives—our Posturepedic mornings, filtered water, iPhones, multi-setting shower heads, and climate-controlled interiors. Summer, August specifically, is meant to remind us of what we're made of. Our armpits should stink, our legs and faces should be unshaven, our beds should be hard, and our creature comforts rudimentary at best.

It's a time to visit family—even the people you can't stand. And visit monuments to human achievement like the Eiffel Tower, as well as monuments to human eccentricity like the Corn Palace of South Dakota.

But we should play games like children, strum a guitar and sing our hearts out, lie bare-assed in the sun, walk barefoot, scratch our mosquito bites with complete abandon, make love under the stars, and really get to know one another again after spending much of the year working and running from appointment to appointment.

"Is that how you spent your summer vacations as a kid?" my husband asked.

"God no," I said. "We loved the American way!"

Please Stay For The Fireworks
(Some Thoughts On Being An American)

My grandparents had close friends—Sonja and Jiri—who hijacked a plane to escape communist Czechoslovakia. Sonja said her hand was shaking so badly that she couldn't have hit a target had she tried. Not that she would have tried—she'd never held a gun before let alone shot one. Until that very day she'd been the pampered wife of a diplomat.

To her relief, the other passengers just sat there, bewildered, and not necessarily upset by the turn of events. After all, they were getting a free ride to a free country and that probably weighed more heavily on their minds than the pretty woman with the trembling fingers and fancy handbag. Sonja and Jiri's defection had forced every person on that flight to make a decision right then and there as to whether they would stay in a new country, leaving their families, their language and their culture behind, or go back to what they knew—even if they didn't like it.

People often underestimate the kind of determination it takes to give up a homeland. To leave behind a sense of belonging that only comes from being born and raised in a specific place. To know that in many cases returning will never be possible—either for political or financial reasons. Think about that. Never.

It is no wonder that immigrants so often make more valued employees and better citizens than their native-born counterparts. My grandfather had been a famous athlete in Czechoslovakia, but there was no factory job too good for him in the U.S. No floor he wouldn't stoop to wash.

And to my knowledge he didn't complain about it, either.

In my family a day of work was never missed and a vote was always cast on election day. Like Sonja and Jiri, my kin had risked their lives to come here and felt a tremendous sense of debt to their adopted homeland. President John F. Kennedy had asked them what they could do for their country and they responded by giving generously to veteran organizations even when they had little extra, sending countless telegrams of support or criticism to various sitting politicians, and by forcing (yes, forcing) my brother to join the ROTC in college. Being a girl, I was not encouraged to join the military—my parents were old fashioned that way. But I was routinely harassed about my civic participation. I don't think I've ever missed an election cycle, no matter how hungover I felt. I even cast absentee ballots when I lived abroad in a semi-permanent hungover state. And I'm an easy target for any legitimate charity that supports policemen, firefighters, and soldiers. I still reflexively cry when I hear "The Star-Spangled Banner."

I think about these things every Fourth of July. How my parents' immigrant status has affected my life and whether I'm sufficiently passing on the values I was taught to my own children.

As you can imagine, the Fourth of July was a very big holiday at my house when I was growing up. Not bigger than Christmas, but definitely paid more attention than our birthdays.

It was the only time my parents would even attempt to barbecue—they hated barbecue. We ate off of red, white, and blue paper plates and sat in traffic for hours to watch some distant fireworks display.

Even whatever bicycle I rode when I was growing up was always required to have some sort of patriotic flair. I remember a bicentennial-themed spectacle complete with a banana seat and long, plastic red, white, and blue streamers that looked like they'd been shot out of my handlebars. Even in the late seventies, that was extremely uncool.

But I knew complaining about it was useless and I kind of look back fondly on that monstrosity of a bike now. It was so damned earnest and earnest patriotism has gone out of fashion.

But I'm trying to bring it back in my own way.

At our house we don't barbecue—my husband hates barbecue far more than my parents ever did—but we make fancy-shmancy cheeseburgers on our gas stove complete with homemade French fries. We lift our kids onto the roof of our minivan to watch the local fireworks display, but living in the country, we're spared the bumper-to-bumper. And now that they're old enough, we've started having conversations with them about what good citizenship means and how important it is to think through the political beliefs they are forming and never be a slave to them.

We don't tell them how we vote and it drives them crazy.

But we think it's important that they form their own opinions and not reflexively embrace or rebel against ours. We've earned ours through trial and error and experience, and they'll have to do the same.

What we do tell them is how important it is to be able to speak freely and make one's own decisions—even if freedom is a burden. Being born in such a highly functioning democracy is like being born on third base, but it is yours to blow. And you don't get a home run just for showing up. Our political system allows class mobility and is amenable to change, and our constitution is both an aspirational and spiritual document—designed to help build and sustain a nation and, uniquely, help its citizens evolve into better human beings, a society of equals free to pursue happiness.

But none of these things comes with a guarantee.

As a good citizen, you have to hold up your end of the bargain and behave with courage, dignity and respect for others.

You must actively contribute, or as our friend, General David Bellon, USMC, would point out, "You either leave a legacy or a residue."

I'm determined to leave the former and do my damnedest to make sure that my children do, too.

The Meaning Of Happiness

My youngest daughter, Josephine, had a birthday this past Friday the 13th.

At seven, she is dreamy, funny, contemplative and just delighted with herself. Typical of her age cohort, she tore apart her wrapping paper with a fiendish glee, strutted around in her brand new mermaid tail (though she has her doubts that mermaids actually exist, she still holds out hope that she can become one, say, as a career or lifestyle choice), and spent half the day talking to herself in the mirror, as she is apt to do.

It was during one of these mirror episodes that she turned to me suddenly and said, "Mom, was the day I was born just the happiest day of your life?"

Huh.

It was not.

The day of her birth and the subsequent few years were by most standards pretty horrible, in fact. Not post-apocalyptic horrible, but bad enough so that I could strike envy off the list of reasons why people didn't like me.

Naturally, I wasn't going to say that. I was also prepared for her question and able to turn to her without missing a beat and say with complete honesty, "You are the best thing that has ever happened to me."

I've written about Josephine's health problems fairly extensively for this collection, so I won't belabor that point.

This post isn't about her fight to survive, but something else entirely.

Her question just got me thinking again about how we define our lives, the decisions we make, and how they affect our long-term well-being. About the struggle between happiness and meaning—something I've given a lot of thought to over the years. Even in those happy-go-lucky years pre-Josephine. The years when our biggest problems revolved around getting a good night's sleep, whether to buy a fixer-upper or a reasonably renovated home, how to lose that last five pounds that pregnancy had visited upon me. Those were very happy years—when my husband and I mostly chased pleasures.

I don't regret a single, frivolous moment.

But even when my husband and I were at the apex of our pursuit of happiness period, there was something about our makeup that wouldn't allow us to try and sustain that sense of bliss on a permanent basis. Plenty of people we knew were willing to do so at any cost—avoiding inconveniences and entanglements like the plague, revolving all of their big decisions, like how many children to have or whether to have any at all, whether to marry or continue living together, around lifestyle.

But then, we were living in California at the time. Sort of comes with the territory.

I actually remember the day I realized we'd somehow lost a deeper sense of service to something other than ourselves. One that was encoded in our DNA by years of Catholic school and family stories of hardship (won't belabor that point either, but it's a theme of mine). The fact is, we were starting to hit the wall on our California experiment.

Don't get me wrong. I know I'm sounding like a

California hater and that's just not true. Some of the best times in my life were spent in the Golden State. My husband and I made dear friends and started our family there. Those are very meaningful things.

But happiness and self-fulfillment are as much a part of the culture there as guilt and shame are a part of Catholicism. And there is a pervasive tendency to find beauty only in beauty.

This was driven home to me one day at the spa.

I'd recently given birth to our first child—a healthy son—and that alone does get the heart juices going. My husband, Jack, being the great husband that he is, bought me an entire spa day at a very swanky San Francisco spa on my very first Mother's Day.

I was beside myself. Really. I couldn't wait to go. I'd given birth, been breast-feeding on what seemed like a round-the-clock basis, and had been up all night for weeks. I needed this desperately.

And for the first hour or so, it was so, so nice. Especially since the day began with a full body massage—which is like chemotherapy for a new mother. Without the un-lovely side effects.

But right in the middle of hour two, during a multi-sensation inducing "ultra" facial, my spa day started to turn on me.

Between the fake sounds of a bubbling brook complete with cawing birds and cricket symphonies, the intermittent New Age muzak, wafts of aromatherapy and what was fast becoming a tyranny of pleasures and pleasantries perpetrated by hush-voiced, toned young men with names like Darius, I thought that if I had to stay for the entire gauntlet of treatments—the ensuing mud bath and hot towel mummification—I might go insane.

But I did stay.

I felt too guilty to cut and run after my husband had given me such a wonderful gift. He'd paid a small fortune just to indulge me. He'd also played Mr. Mom all day with our infant son without a complaint, passive aggressive comment or hint about the standing ovation he should receive for his efforts. He is an enormously competent and fully grown-up man, which is one of the many things I love about him.

I also love that he fully understood when I told him about my day.

And that understanding began a discussion that would wrench us from our glamorous city lives in San Francisco and deliver us to a town that wasn't exactly Mayberry, but was certainly slow, pastoral and grounded in tradition. A place that was more equipped to help us through the hardships we'd be facing in the coming years—when our happy lives would come to a crashing halt. At least for a while.

Because when I elaborated about my dreadful too-much-of-a-good-thing spa experience, my husband got very pensive. He nodded and looked out of our rear window—where the opera singer practiced her arias, gourmet margaritas were consumed on a nightly basis, and the grass on our tiny patch of backyard was Astroturf-perfect and surrounded by bougainvillea. He said, "You know, I think we're going to have to re-evaluate our lives."

That spa day was an incredible event of foreshadowing. In the years to come we would be needing much more than happiness if we were going to be happy. Endlessly chasing the dragon of happiness can lead to a great time had, but it can also leave a person ill-prepared to continue to feel well during more profound periods of heartache. If there's nothing of real meaning under-girding a lifestyle, it becomes all too easy to fall prey to a toxic cocktail of self-pity and depression when the big stuff happens.

We knew on an instinctive level—almost as if we had some inkling that Josephine was headed our way—that it was imperative for us to deepen our faith and find greater purpose—joy, even—in something other than a fun, uncomplicated existence.

In our post-fabulous years, we've settled in a small college town in central Virginia. We help groom the grounds at the monastery where we go to church, we volunteer at the local hospital—giving speeches about parent perspectives to young nurses and residents—and we stay in most nights. We should probably go out more. But we do mix great cocktails that we drink nightly on our porch, we have friends over as often as we can, and we hit the beach every year.

We hardly think about what things were like "before" anymore, although recently I got a little taste.

Last week, I visited San Francisco for a wonderful week of friendship, food, and wine in honor of one of my very best friends' significant birthdays. It was a week of both happiness and meaning as a group of seven women laughed and talked and shared about both painful and frivolous events.

I walked around San Francisco, which appears to have become decidedly more family-friendly since our time, and observed young couples who were just as we had been—a mom pushing a stroller with a sun-drunk toddler in it, a dad sporting an infant carrier complete with a hazy-eyed newborn, the color of his irises yet indeterminable.

I admit I felt nostalgic for those times. We were different people then, ones whose peace of mind had yet to be broken not just into shards, but ground to dust. Our younger selves didn't fully know how good we had it or how bad things could really get.

But at the same time, I felt a profound sense of relief that those footloose days were behind us. Our decrease in happiness has come with an unwavering confidence in ourselves both as individuals and as a couple.

We know what we're made of now.

And we have some wisdom to impart to our children. Something to give to friends who are struggling. And a list of priorities that doesn't begin with achievements or desires.

We love more deeply and when we dance, we mean it. Most counterintuitively, we've recaptured a teenage ideal of true love and loyalty while having acquired an adult sense of forgiveness and good judgment.

It's a great life. And it's a life filled with meaning, if not always happiness. And that's a fine place to be.

Victoria Dougherty

Victoria Dougherty is the author of The Bone Church. She writes fiction, drama and essays that revolve around lovers, killers, curses and destinies.

Her work has been published or profiled in the New York Times, USA Today, The International Herald Tribune and elsewhere.

Her blog – COLD – features her short essays on faith, family, love and writing. WordPress, the blogging platform that hosts some 72 million blogs worldwide has singled out COLD as one of the top 50 Recommended Blogs on writers and writing.

Currently, Ms. Dougherty lives with her family in Charlottesville, VA and has recently completed The Hungarian, her second in a series of Cold War themed historical thrillers.

Follow COLD at www.victoriadougherty.wordpress.com

Spies. Lovers. Curses. Destinies. From the author of *The Bone Church* and *Cold*, comes a white knuckle tour de force of Cold War noir.

Get your free copy here:
http://victoriadoughertybooks.com/heres-your-free-book/

What people are saying about *The Bone Church* by Victoria Dougherty:

"In this case heavy is good. Very good."—*Back Porchervations*

"The Bone Church is possibly one of the darkest and most sophisticated historical novels you'll be able to put your hands on." —Mina DeCaro, *Mina's Bookshelf*

"This novel has it all . . . an addictive jaunt into a world of paranoia, deceit, mistrust and then the ultimate betrayal. I really, really, really loved this book."—*The Lit Bitch*

www.ingramcontent.com/pod-product-compliance
Lightning Source LLC
Chambersburg PA
CBHW032105090426
42743CB00007B/243